CRUISING THROUGH THE PANAMA CANAL
REVISED FOR 2018-19

CONTENTS

INTRODUCTION

One of the most popular cruise itineraries is the transit of the Panama Canal on a journey between Los Angeles or San Francisco, California and either Miami or Fort Lauderdale, Florida. For many a transit through the Panama Canal fulfills a lifetime dream, as there is no other canal on earth as famous or that symbolizes as much as does this man-made wonder, opened in 1914. Other cruise itineraries include a transit through the canal, especially on the route between the west coast of South America and Florida or as part of an around the world cruise. Some cruise lines also offer an end of season repositioning cruise between Vancouver, Canada and Florida at the start of the fall or spring seasons to prepare for the Caribbean or Alaska season. More details regarding itineraries will be presented in the next chapter

A CRUISE THROUGH THE CANAL: Today the standard cruise between Florida and California takes around two weeks to 16 days depending on the specific itinerary. And for the majority of passengers the highlight or crown jewel of the voyage is the transit of the Panama Canal. It takes anywhere from seven to nine hours to cross between the two oceans, and for cruise ships it is always a daylight passage so that passengers can see close up the workings of the locks and enjoy the tropical scenery and activity of the man-made lake and cut through the Continental Divide. I have made the crossing four times and each transit was as exciting as the very first. It is hard for the Panama Canal to loose its magic.

The best time of the year to book such a cruise is between late November and the end of April. The weather is difficult to predict, but during the Northern Hemisphere winter, even in these tropical latitudes, temperatures are slightly lower, generally in the low to mid 20's Celsius or mid 80's Fahrenheit. And the humidity levels are also lower despite the chance for rain occurring on more than half of the days. But it is not likely that you will experience an entire day of rain, as the weather patterns are such that brief thundershowers are the norm. But during the Northern Hemisphere summer months, this area comes under the threat of hurricanes on both the Caribbean and Pacific coasts, and for that reason plus the added heat and humidity cruise lines do not schedule Panama Canal crossings.

When you look at the physical geography of the Americas, the North American continent narrows down to only100 kilometers or 60 miles at the Isthmus of Panama, yet building a canal was a difficult undertaking in the late 19th and early 20th centuries. Tropical conditions and rough topography created what at the time were almost insurmountable problems. Prior to the building of a canal, there was only one alternative in traveling between the Atlantic and Pacific Oceans. That alternative was a lengthy journey around the bottom of South America, adding over 8,000 miles to a journey between the east coast of the United States or Canada and the west coast. At the bottom of the continent, the Straits of Magellan became the safest passage, yet it has narrow spots and swift currents, necessitating the use of local pilots. The only open ocean passage is around the very tip of land's end, which is Cape Horn. Here the prevailing westerly winds howl at speeds up to and sometimes in excess of 160 kilometers or 100 miles per hour. In the days of sailing vessels, it was virtually impossible to make the passage unscathed. Captain Bligh of the famous ship HMS Bounty tried sailing west for over a month before turning back and crossing the Atlantic to Cape Town where he had to put in for repairs. Even today's modern vessels replete with sophisticated stabilizers and powerful engines find navigating through the Drake Passage a treacherous journey, undertaken only during the summer months and even then only when conditions are optimum. Many cruise itineraries that include rounding the cape often find it necessary to detour through the southerly Beagle Channel, missing the opportunity to see land's end.

This traveler's companion is designed for those visitors who are planning a cruise that will transit the Panama Canal. It will provide you with information regarding the major ports of call in both oceans as well as detailed descriptions of the Panama Canal and its workings. The material on the transit through the canal is presented twice, once for those who will experience the passage from the Caribbean to the Pacific and once for those traveling from the Pacific to the Caribbean, as the journeys are essentially different.

I trust that this traveler's companion will be beneficial in helping you to become acquainted with the landscapes, history and cultures of the countries to be visited. And you come to gain an understanding of the building of the canal and its significance today along with its present limitations. In this updated edition, I have added some specific recommendations as to shopping and dining out. My recommendations are based upon presenting the highest quality establishments given that in many of these ports the level of health and sanitation is not what most of us expect. It is always better to be careful than sorry when it comes to watching where and what you eat. This is not a typical guidebook such as Fyodor's or Frommer's. You will not find pages of restaurant or hotel recommendations, but rather brief descriptions of the ports of call, showing you their major highlights. And the recommendations are few in number, but giving you the finest choices available. The primary focus is to offer you an overall introduction to the lands and peoples you will be seeing. By reading this book you will have gained a very good working knowledge of the historic and cultural details of each place to be visited.

Lew Deitch
January 2018

Visit my web site for other publications
and a beautiful around the world slide show
http://www.doctorlew.com

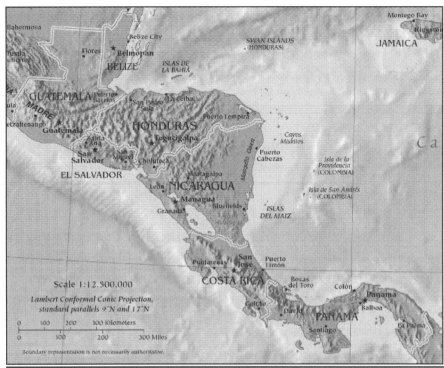

A General Physical Political Map of Central America

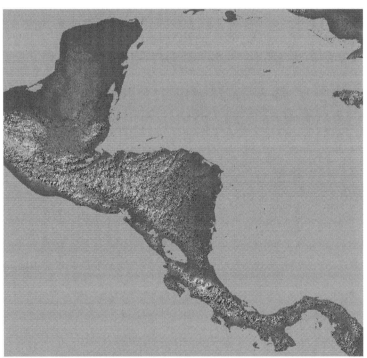

Topographic map of Central America

PREPARING TO CRUISE

For those of us living in North America or Europe, there is a certain mystique about the Panama Canal. The actual transit occupies the better part of one day, thus most cruises include ports of call on either side of the canal to generate an itinerary that entices people to book. There is essentially one route, but the possibility for a variety of stops to be made. The majority of the Panama Canal cruises are between southern Florida and the west coast of the United States, with much longer cruises between eastern and western Canada. The following list presents the primary itineraries used by the major cruise lines that include a transit of the canal:

* Miami or Fort Lauderdale - Los Angeles or San Francisco
* Miami or Fort Lauderdale - San Diego
* Miami or Fort Lauderdale to Vancouver (spring repositioning)
* Vancouver to Miami or Fort Lauderdale (fall repositioning)
* Vancouver to Montréal (fall repositioning)
* Miami or Fort Lauderdale to Valparaiso, Chile
* Valparaiso, Chile to Miami or Fort Lauderdale

The individual ports of call may vary slightly from one cruise line to another, but the deviations are minor. The following list starting on the Atlantic side presents the major ports of call that can be included in a Panama Canal itinerary:

* Cartagena, Colombia
* Puerto Limón, Costa Rica (Atlantic)
* San Blas Islands, Panama
* Colón, Panama
* Panama City, Panama
* Limón, Costa Rica
* Puntarenas, Costa Rica
* Puerto Quetzal, Guatemala
* Puerto Chiapas, México
* Acapulco, México
* Manzanilla, México
* Zihuatanejo & Ixtapa, México
* Puerto Vallarta, México
* Cabo San Lucas, México

This traveler's guide has been prepared for those who are planning a cruise that will transit the Panama Canal. As previously noted, it is designed to provide you with geographic and historic information so that you become better informed about the major places you will be visiting. It will also describe in detail the transit of the Panama Canal in both westbound and eastbound modes. But unlike a traditional guidebook, it is not designed to provide extensive restaurant or hotel listings, but rather only the top establishments. For that type of detail, you need to consult either Frommer's or Fyodor's guidebooks.

PREPARING TO CRUISE: What do you need to do to prepare for your cruise? This question involves numerous sub topics that will be explained. There are many questions people have regarding visas, the flights, what to pack with regard to weather conditions, currency issues and health concerns. I will address many of those issues here. If you have specific and personalized questions, please contact me at my web page through the "Ask Doctor Lew" page. I will respond with answers to your personal questions. The web site is http://www.doctorlew.com.

VISAS: For citizens holding United States, Canadian or European Union passports, no visas are required for the ports of call on the many itineraries offered by the various cruise lines. If, however, you plan to leave the ship in México, a tourist visa would be necessary. But I have found that it is rare that someone will plan to leave the ship in one of the Mexican ports of call. For holders of passports from countries other than those stated here, it will be necessary to check with the cruise line to see if visas are required.

FLIGHTS TO AND FROM THE SHIP: For those of you living in North America, flights to or from Miami, Fort Lauderdale or Los Angeles are varied, but quite numerous. All three cities have direct flights or single connections to all major airports within the United States and Canada. If you are sailing on one of the Canadian relocation cruises, there are direct flights between major cities in the United States and both Vancouver and Montréal.

Flights from European cities such as London, Paris, Frankfurt or Zurich take around 14 hours to the west coast and around eight to nine hours to Miami, and flying westward, you loose time. I highly recommend Business Class because most airlines today offer the full flat beds, which are so much more comfortable than being in coach or even the upgraded coach class. Yes it is more expensive, but there are non-refundable Business Class fares if you purchase well ahead of traveling. And some cruise lines may offer special Business Class travel included with your cruise.

WEATHER: For Panama Canal sailings, you will be in tropical waters most of the time. The daily weather will be warm and humid. Temperatures will be in the mid 20's Celsius or 80's Fahrenheit and humidity levels can be anywhere from 70 to as high as 90 percent, especially in Panama. Rainfall varies, but during the December to February period, late morning or afternoon thundershowers are relatively common. It is less common to have a full day of rain during most sailings. However, if you are doing an eastbound repositioning cruise in September, there is always the possibility of either a Pacific or Atlantic hurricane. But the cruise lines keep a close watch on the weather and will not steer the ship into any uncomfortable situations.

WHAT TO PACK: You will be well advised to pack light clothes, preferably cotton in pastel colors, as they breathe easier and help keep you cool. If you are prone to any adverse reaction to heat or sunlight, a comfortable hat is recommended. And it is also wise to have a good sunscreen. For those planning daytime outings into the tropical rainforest, insect repellant is also recommended.

Depending upon your cruise line, you may need formal or smart casual dress for evening events on board. This of course varies with each cruise operator. And attending such evening events is always optional.

On deck, a light sweater or windbreaker is advisable, especially once the ship sails into temperate latitudes. The California coast can be relatively cool during the winter months. And if you are on a repositioning cruise between Canadian ports in the autumn, warmer sweaters or jackets will be necessary for maximum comfort. Likewise a lightweight raincoat or poncho is also recommended on the Canadian portions of the cruise as well as for touring into the tropical rainforests of Central America or the Caribbean.

CURRENCY: In most ports of call most local merchants or restaurants will accept internationally recognized credit cards. However, street vendors and smaller merchants may be unwilling to accept American or Canadian Dollars or Euro. Changing money into local currency is often not practical, especially if you are going on a ship sponsored tour. But if you plan to go off on your own in any of the ports, especially if you plan to hire a local taxi, it is essential to have sufficient currency of that country.

My recommendation is to order small amounts of local currency from your bank at home prior to departure.

POSTAGE: If you wish to send post cards or letters you are best doing it on board the ship. But even in so doing, there is only a fifty percent chance that the mail will be received at its final destination. The postal systems are not that reliable when it comes to international mail except in Costa Rica. You will be better served using e-mail.

FOOD AND WATER: Countries in Central America have a notorious reputation for being places in which it is easy to become ill from food and water. It is always better to be safe than sorry, as some food or water borne bacteria can cause you long term, serious problems such as hepatitis or worse. México has the worst reputation for what is sometimes euphemistically called "Montezuma's Revenge." The same would be true for Guatemala and Colombia. If you eat in reputable restaurants and do not eat any raw foods, you lessen the odds of becoming sick by a significant factor.

Always drink bottled water, preferably taken with you from the ship. If you buy bottled water onshore make certain that the bottles are properly sealed. It is not recommended to eat raw vegetables, especially salads unless you are in a major international hotel or five-star restaurant. Fruits that can be pealed are safe to eat, but for added insurance, it is better if you peal the fruit.

Do not eat from street vendors or small local restaurants, as the level of sanitation is highly questionable even though the food may have been cooked. Remember that the local inhabitants are accustomed to the conditions and their bodies have already developed a resistance to various bacteria or parasites that we have no immunity to.

Of all the countries being visited, the highest standards of cleanliness are to be found in Costa Rica, especially in the major cities and towns. But even here it is still advisable to eat only in restaurants that appear to be of high quality. There is far less danger of becoming ill in Costa Rica except in Limón, which is on the tropical Caribbean coast. It is a good idea to have your doctor prescribe Lomotil and Cipro as a precaution.

HEALTH CONCERNS: There are no special vaccinations required for the ports of call on a Panama Canal cruise. Although mosquitos can be pesky at times in the rainforest, there is no danger of the transmission of malaria or yellow fever in the places you will be visiting.

Always take out a traveler's health insurance policy before departure from home. And make certain that you have a sizable allowance for medical evacuation. This is just a normal precaution when traveling in areas where the local medical services do not meet the standards you are accustomed to.

Costa Rica is the one country in Central America where medical services meet the standards we normally expect. In fact, many North American women fly to Costa Rica to have cosmetic surgery in licensed clinics that charge far less than in the United States or Canada.

CRIME: Street crime is a problem in some of the ports of call, especially purse snatching and pickpockets. Just observe the normal precautions you would in many parts of the world. And for added safety do not wear expensive jewelry or watches and do not show large sums of money when making any transactions. This is just a wise precaution.

You no doubt have read about extreme drug violence in Colombia. Once again, these reports often lead one to believe that you will not be safe when visiting. Colombia has seen major police and military action to reign in the role of the drug cartels, and they have been very successful. Cartagena is a very safe city for visitors, especially in the historic old city where most of the sights are located. I have personally explored much of the city and have always felt very safe. There is a strong police presence, especially in areas visited by tourists.

Costa Rica has a very high standard of living and petty crimes are minimal. This is without question the safest country in Central America. Its overall violent crime rate is very low as are petty street crimes. But it is still recommended to take normal precautions regarding jewelry and money.

In recent years Guatemala has seen an upsurge in violent crime, especially with the drug cartels now using its more remote areas. If you visit Antigua or any of the Maya ruins on one of the ship's tours, you will be perfectly safe, but it is advisable during free time to remain in well-patronized public areas.

México is still experiencing high crime in many areas of the country where the drug cartels are active. And many of the reports are alarming. Of all the ports being visited, the only one in which you need to be especially careful is Acapulco. This is a major city of over 2,000,000 and it has seen its share of excessive violence. It is best in Acapulco to only leave the ship as part of an organized tour or with a private car and driver arranged through the cruise line. Venturing out on your own varies as to the level of safety dependent upon recent local events. On one visit a few years back, there had just been a shootout in the street in front of the cruise terminal two days before the ship arrived. As a result, there was a very high police presence and I did take a small group on a walking tour with no incident.

COLOMBIA AS A NATION

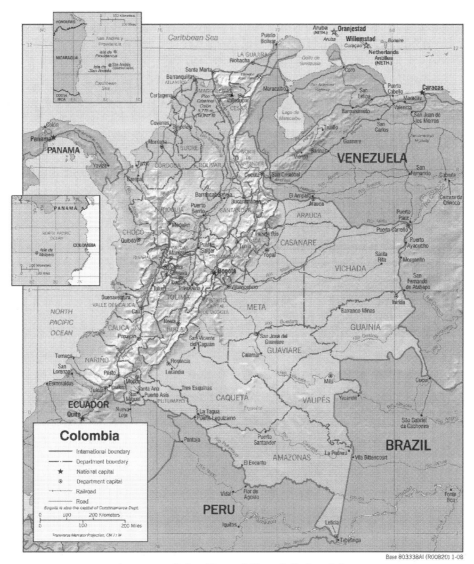

A map of the Republic of Colombia

Colombia is a large country occupying 1,141,666 square kilometers or 440,800 square miles and having a population of just over 48,000,000. It is located at the northwestern corner of South America and is the only country on the continent to have two coastlines, this because of the narrow Isthmus of Panama, which borders Colombia. Its longer coast extending south of Panama is on the Pacific Ocean while its lesser coast is on the Caribbean Sea, an arm of the Atlantic Ocean. The coastal plains are relatively narrow

13

and they have a hot, humid climate with thick rainforest growth. There are several ribs of the Andes Mountains with high intervening valleys that make up the core of the country where most people live. Elevations for valleys are as high as 2,438 meters or 8,000 feet and peaks extend as high as 4,877 meters or 16,000 feet. Bogotá, the nation's capital is the highest city of over 3,050 meters or 10,000,000 in the world. Beyond the mountains with their cool valleys and forested slopes is the Amazon Basin, which is a hot and sultry tropical rainforest extending all the way east to the Atlantic Ocean. Remember that the high Andes Mountains begin in northern Venezuela (to the east) and run through the heart of Colombia. There are many highly active volcanoes in the Andes of Colombia. And numerous severe earthquakes frequent this region. Yet the country's major cities of Bogotá, Cali and Medellin are all located in the highlands because it is far more comfortable climatically despite the greater earthquake danger. And many smaller towns and cities are within the danger zone of numerous of the country's active volcanoes.

Cartagena, the port visited by most cruise ships is located on the Caribbean coast, fronting both on the open ocean and a large interior bay. It is a hot, tropical city and the natural environment figures very much into its architecture and lifestyle. And it is located in a region that does not experience the dangers of earthquakes or hurricanes as well. Being a city on the Caribbean coast, one would think that there would be a high frequency of hurricanes. The track of Atlantic hurricanes rarely brings them along the Colombian northern coast, rarely ever coming as far south as Cartagena. .

Colombia, named for Christopher Columbus, is an old country. The Spanish first arrived in 1499, conquering or killing most native peoples and creating the Viceroyalty of New Granada. During the colonial era, there was much exploitation of those natives that survived, and through interbreeding the bulk of the population today claims both native and Spanish blood. Spain was more concerned with gold, silver and emeralds along with the saving of souls. It even established a branch of the Inquisition in Cartagena to root out pagan and heretical beliefs.

The people of Colombia ultimately rebelled against Spain and gained independence in 1819. Initially Gran Colombia included

Venezuela and Ecuador, but they chose their own paths by 1830. After internal strife, corruption and autocratic rule, Colombia emerged in 1886 as a republic and it has been relatively successful in maintaining democratic ideals to the present. However, it went through a terribly violent period where drug cartels and a secessionist movement created great unrest, much violence and death. At one point, Bogotá was the most violent capital in the world.

Today Colombia wears its ethnic diversity quite proudly with native, mestizo, African and European roots living side by side. Adding to this mix has been some recent immigration from Europe and the Middle East. The country is still quite agrarian, with coffee and sugar cane being two great cash crops. Gold and emeralds are still mined in large quantities. And the major cities do show degrees of manufacturing and industrial development. And unfortunately the export of cocaine is still a factor in the underground economy.

VISITING CARTAGENA

A map of greater Cartagena (© OpenStreetMap contributors)

Cartagena de Indias, Colombia is the largest city and port on the country's Caribbean coast. The city of Cartagena is large, with a population of 1,239,000 people. It is also very old and historic at the same time as being very new and dynamic. It blends both worlds together into one exciting and vibrant city.

The Caribbean coast of Colombia is well within tropical latitudes and experiences a very warm and humid climate with frequent afternoon thundershowers. May through June and October through November are the two rainiest times of the year. Thus most cruise ships visit in the period late November to early May when conditions are at their best, but still quite warm and humid to where many of us feel discomfort.

The surrounding countryside is covered in thick woodland with pockets of old growth rainforest. Given its high population, the hinterland around Cartagena is well populated with farms and plantations raising a wide variety of tropical fruits for both local consumption and export. Coffee, for which Colombia is so famous, is not raised in the coastal region near Cartagena, but rather in the mountainous highlands, which dominate the west central portion of the country.

ARRIVING IN PORT: It takes over an hour to sail into the port at Cartagena even though you will see a large opening in the bay adjacent to the city called Boca Grande. Despite meaning wide mouth, in early Spanish colonial times a subsurface wall of stone was created to keep enemy fleets from easily sailing into the harbor. Thus all ships were and still are required to enter through the smaller southern gap known as Boca Chica where Bateria San José and Fuerte San Fernando could open a hail of fire to destroy any would be invader. It is impressive today to sail past these now quiet historic forts, then through the clear blue waters and see the dramatic skyline of the city emerge on the horizon. Cartagena has several areas of impressive high-rises that stand in contrast with its historic districts.

A RICH HISTORY: Native settlement can be dated as far back as 9,000 years ago, showing that this rich coastal plain had long been valued for its capability of supporting a hunting, gathering and limited farming society.

Pedro de Heredia founded the port of Cartagena de Indias in 1533, named after the parent city of Cartagena on the Spanish Mediterranean coast. It soon became an important and rich trade center with discoveries of gold in the interior and with its potential for raising sugar cane. French pirates operating in the Caribbean pillaged the port in 1544 and 1563, followed by a British privateer's attempt to capture the city in 1568.

The famous British seaman Sir Francis Drake managed to capture and plunder Cartagena in 1574, and was ultimately paid a hefty ransom by the Spanish crown in order to get him to leave the city. It was as a result of these repeated attacks that the Spanish government began to heavily fortify the port in the early 17th century, including the building of the sub surface wall across Boca Grande. The crowning achievement was the building of the massive Castillo San Felipe de Barajas on a hill overlooking the city, which also became enclosed in a massive wall. Today both the old city and the Castillo along with the two forts at the entry to Boca Chica and several other monuments are all UNESCO World Heritage sites.

Despite the fortifications, raids upon Cartagena continued to be harassed. And in 1697, the French were successful in capturing the city and destroying much of its infrastructure. By 1711, with the end of the War of the Spanish Succession, and the restoration of military control, the Castillo was greatly strengthened because it had fallen to the French in the Raid on Cartagena in 1697.

The most audacious attack came in 1741 when British Admiral Edward Vernon mounted a land invasion, landing troops to attempt a capture of the city. The Spanish forces were able to repel the invaders and the city was not captured. But an interesting side note of historic importance is that George Washington's half brother served with Admiral Vernon and was so impressed with his bravery and audacity. This ultimately prompted George Washington to name his plantation in Virginia Mount Vernon in honor of the admiral.

During the 18th century, Cartagena reached its pinnacle of wealth, being the center for export of gold, silver, emeralds, sugar and coffee. It was during this period that many magnificent churches and palatial homes along with beautiful public buildings were erected inside the walled city. Today these constitute the most historic and visited portion of the city by tourists who come in the tens of thousands, mostly by cruise ship.

On a darker side, the Spanish crown established the Inquisition Holy Office Court in Cartagena in 1610 to root out infidels and those unfaithful to the Catholic Church. The inquisition office came complete with instruments of torture that are still on display to the present. The Palace of the Inquisition functioned until 1811 when Cartagena declared its independence from Spanish rule. For two centuries, the palace was one of three centers of inquisition in the Spanish Americas.

The revolutionary war that followed the declaration of independence from Spain nearly destroyed Cartagena when a Spanish expeditionary force captured it in 1816. In 1821 patriots recaptured the city after a siege of 159 days, but it left much of the city in ruin and Cartagena's importance as a port began to wane. This was followed by famine and cholera, further weakening the city. The road to recovery after Colombian independence was slow and by the early 20th century, the city once again became an important port.

CARTAGENA TODAY: Today tourism plays a major role in the economy, as does heavy industry. Cartagena is an important container port for cities in the interior. It is also a center for the manufacturing of chemicals and the refining of petroleum. Toe encourage manufacturing, the Colombian government has established several tax free zones around Cartagena that have helped bring in further manufacturing activity.

But tourism has shown the greatest impact upon the city. Many wealthy Colombians have made this a favored beach resort, building lavish homes or buying into the massive high-rise condos built along a narrow strip of land called Boca Grande, the strip being essentially the result of dredging the bay. Today this is the first sight you see, as your ship sails into the harbor. Boca Grande is only a couple of blocks wide, its northern shore washed by the Caribbean and its backside facing the inner harbor. On this strip of about two miles in length the skyline is one of wall-to-wall high-rises of impressive height. However, because of strong winds of the Caribbean, a plan to build a 58-story high-rise, tallest in Colombia, was dropped. Most of the hotels and apartments on Boca Grande are under 30 stories, but their mass is what is impressive. It lends an ultra-modern note, especially being adjacent to the wall of the old, historic city.

What is there to see in Cartagena? Most cruise passengers choose one of the tours of the city offered by the cruise line. Remember that this is a large city of well over a million people. But most of the historic sites are in and around the Old City near where the ship will dock. Some cruise lines do offer a shuttle bus that normally drops passengers at the famous Clock Tower along the wall where one of the major gates is located. Is it safe to go off on your own? The answer is a resounding yes. The government considers Cartagena to be a showplace and is proud of its developing tourist industry. Police maintain a strong presence in and around the Old City, and thus visitors can feel quite safe. However, keep in mind that not all merchants and vendors speak English. You are on the northern shore of South America, far from the United States or Canada, and thus English is not as widely spoken. If you have a working knowledge of Spanish you can navigate around with greater confidence. This is why I strongly urge most passengers to sign up for one of the ship's tours. You will see the highlights of Cartagena in the company of a guide and will therefore learn more about the city's rich past, the architecture you will be seeing and the overall flavor.

If you have an adventurous nature such as I do, and if you have a working knowledge of Spanish then you can either hire a taxi providing you can communicate or you can arrange for a private car and driver through your shore excursion office. I have toured around every part of Cartagena, and have found it very interesting. There is a massive open air market district that covers many blocks, selling food, clothing, furniture and just about anything people with limited incomes can need. It is very crowded and for some visitors it could be a bit intimidating. Farther south into the main residential heart of the city there are a couple of nice shopping centers that cater strictly to local people, but with more affluence. Exito is the largest retail outlet in Cartagena, and there are a few of their massive stores that anyone who truly wants to explore another culture will find very interesting.

Cartagena has many middle income and more affluent residential districts where both single-family homes and apartment blocks are interspersed with local parks and sports fields. Once again it is safe to take a walk through one of these neighborhoods either alone or with your driver simply to capture the local flavor of daily Colombian life.

And on the northern bay that faces the international airport there are some very depressed barrios where the poorest people live. It is sad to see that a segment of the population lives in makeshift houses built out of whatever scrap material they can salvage. These neighborhoods have no running water, electricity or sewage disposal. And of course it would not be advisable to view these areas except from a distance simply because visitors with cameras would be considered invasive, and you would not be welcomed.

THE MAJOR HIGHLIGHTS: Most visitors will want to concentrate on the major highlights of Cartagena. Guided tours offered by the cruise line will insure that you see as many of the major highlights as possible on either four-hour or full day tours. All of the sites I list are open during daylight hours seven days per week, especially when cruise ships are visiting. The list below represents my recommendations as to the major sights not to be missed, but knowing it will not be possible to do them all:

* The Walled City - This is the heart of any visit to Cartagena and most cruise tours will take you on a guided walk through the Old City
* Castillo San Felipe de Barajas - The massive fortress overlooking the city is the true highlight of Cartagena. Its thick walls and battlements are especially impressive as are the views from the top of its ramparts. It is open daily and you can visit on your own or in a group.
* Cerro la Popa and Convento de la Popa - The best vantage point for a sweeping view over the entire city of Cartagena. The convent is also a very historic and beautiful old building worthy of note. You do need a car or taxi to reach this summit on your own.
* Plaza Santo Domingo - The main plaza in the heart of the Old City. There are many outdoor cafes where a cold beer or soft drink can be purchased, but be sure to not order anything containing ice just as a precaution. The plaza is open daily and is very colorful.
* Plaza Bolivar - The other primary plaza, heavily shaded and containing the major statue of Simon Bolivar, liberator of much of the Andean region of South America from Spain. This plaza is open daily and is very popular among locals.
* Palacio de la Inquision - To appreciate the history of the Spanish Inquisition and see many of the instruments of torture, this is an important venue, but not the happiest of themes.
* Catedral de San Pedro de Claver - A cathedral and monastery dedicated to one of the early priests who ministered to slaves during the era of Spanish slavery
* St Catherine of Alexander Cathedral - One of the most beautiful of the cathedrals in the center of the Old City
* Getsemani - One of the older neighborhoods outside of the wall of the Old City, slightly seedy and a bit ramshackle but filled with very popular local nightclubs and restaurants. But only attempt to dine if you are with a local guide who knows the food scene
* Museo Naval de Caribe - This is the best naval museum in which to learn about the Spanish role in the Caribbean
* Boca Grande - It is a must to drive through or even park and walk in Bocagrande, the modern and rather "glitzy" beachfront strip that dominates the Cartagena skyline

These are just the highlights of sights to see in Cartagena. With only a short time to visit, if you manage to see half of the sites listed above you will have done quite well. Cartagena is the type of city that many visitors wish to return to, as it is filled with beautiful architecture and exudes an inviting image of what an Old Spanish colonial city should look like. I have visited numerous times and have enjoyed exploring not only the city, but also some of the beaches well outside of the city along with some of the neighboring villages. But of course it cannot be done during a one-day port call.

DINING OUT: If you are on an all day tour, it will include lunch. But if you are doing a half-day tour or out on your own, you may wish to sample local cuisine. There are numerous restaurants in the Old City and in Centro as well as out in the suburban areas, but you need to be very careful with regard to the issue of health. Sanitation levels are not what most of us are accustomed to, and the nature of the food, spices and preparation techniques is quite different. Thus caution should be the guide. Do not eat raw vegetables or have a salad just to be safe. And if you eat any fresh fruit, make certain it has been pealed. I am only recommending a few choice restaurants based upon personal knowledge, as I am always overly cautious.

Here are my choices for Cartagena, and they feature traditional Colombian dishes:
* El Baron - Located on Carrera 4 # 31-7 on Plaza de San Pedro Claver, this is a very highly popular establishment open for lunch and dinner between Noon and 2 AM, Tuesday thru Saturday and 5 PM to 1 AM on Sunday and Monday. You can dine with confidence in the quality, freshness and preparation of your lunch. The menu is a mix of North and South American cuisines served in a gastropub atmosphere.
* La Cocina de Pepina - In Gesmani at Calle 25 # 9a-06, this is an outstanding restaurant for lunch or dinner. It serves lunch between Noon and 4 PM and dinner from 7 to 9:30 PM Tuesday thru Saturday with only lunch served from Noon to 4 PM Sunday and Monday. The cuisine is traditional Colombian and Caribbean with seafood figuring prominently. They pride themselves in using fresh ingredients and will tell you that it is safe to eat all of their food, but I still prefer to use caution.
* Restaurante 1621 - Located in the old city at Carrera 7 and Calle del Curato and open only for dinner starting at 7 until 11 PM. This is only accessible if your ship is staying late into the evening. This is an outstanding restaurant featuring cuisine representing all of northern South America and it is served in an elegant atmosphere.

* Caffe Lunatico - In the city center at Calle Espiritu Santo # 29-184, this rather off beat looking cafe has excellent food with a true Colombian flavor. They serve a variety of traditional entrees, offer fresh fruit juices and everything is fresh. Lunch is served daily from 11 AM to 3 PM and dinner from 7 to 10 PM Monday thru Saturday.

SHOPPING: As this will most likely be your only port city in Colombia, many of you will be interested in buying some local crafts. Colombia is a nation that still prides itself in fine artisans who do outstanding weaving, wood carving and create elegant ceramics. And for those wanting to spend a lot of money, the major item to focus upon is the emerald. Colombia is the world's leading producer of gem quality emeralds and there are many shops specializing in these elegant gems. But you must be careful to make sure you are in a reputable shop. Some cruise lines have a personal shopper on board who will often organize small groups of those guests who are looking to buy Colombian emeralds.

I am recommending the following places to shop for quality Colombian arts and crafts, not the large shopping malls of which there are three in Cartagena. I will start with one listing I know to be reputable with regard to emeralds:
* Lucy Jewelry - Located at Calle Santo Domingo #3-19 near the Plaza Santo Domingo, this magnificent store has a good reputation for honesty and quality, two factors very important when buying emeralds. Open daily from 9 AM to 8 PM, closed Sunday.
* Colombia Artesanal - Located at Calle de los Escribos # a-104 in the old city historic district, this shop specializes in fine quality Colombian arts and crafts by well-recognized masters. Open 9 AM to 11 PM daily.
* NH Galeria - At Carrera 2 # 33-36, this is a fine quality gallery featuring Colombian art of a contemporary era with recognized artists. Open 20 AM to 8 PM Monday thru Saturday and 4 to 8 PM on Sunday.
* Las Bovedas - Located in the Old City along Carrera 2 at the north end, this one time collection of jail cells that run for over a block in length. Each former cell is now a craft store, but you will only find mass-produced items of lower, less expensive quality. This is very much of a tourist oriented shopping experience and I only mention it because there are many of you just looking for souvenir items. Open 7 AM to 8 PM daily.

* Chino Market Area - Located along Avenida Pedro de Heredia, this is not a place to go shopping, but rather to explore where the locals shop in a chaotic series of streets lined with small shops. Do not go without a guide, as it would not be the safest place for anyone with a camera. But if you want local color, this is the place.

FINAL WORDS: Cartagena has mad great strides in presenting a safe atmosphere for visitors. You will notice a strong police presence, and in the five times I have visited I was never approached by an unsavory characters and never felt uncomfortable even in many of the non-tourist oriented neighborhoods. Yes Colombia has a notorious reputation for drug violence, but much of that was centered in the interior around places like Medellin and Cali, not Cartagena. But even in the major interior cities, the government has made great strides in curbing the public violence and even those cities are relatively safe for visitors.

You will find that Old Cartagena has some of the most beautiful Old Spanish colonial architecture to be found anywhere in the Americas. And the city residents are taking great pride in showing it off to visitors. This is a city of contrasts between old and new, rich and poor, and it is vibrant.

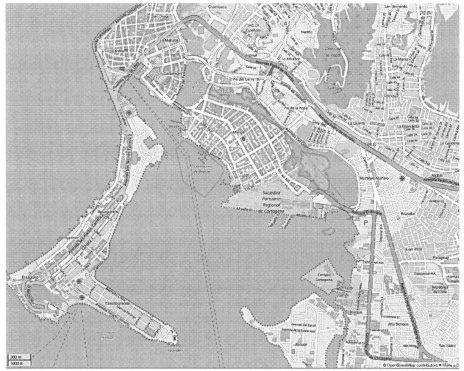

A map of the heart of Cartagena (© OpenStreetMap contributors)

A view from Cerro la Popa across to Bocagrande

The skyline of Boca Grande

Castillo San Felipe, the great fortress

On the streets of Old Cartagena so full of life

Old Cartagena has the feel of Colonial Spain

A fruit vendor at the Plaza Bolivar in Old Cartagena

El Teatro Heredia in Old Cartagena

A special folk dance performance on the steps of Teatro Heredia

A student outing in Bolivar Plaza in Old Cartagena

In the heart of Centro, the downtown core of Cartagena

The chaotic nature of the Chino Market area

Daily life on the streets of La Concepcion in the lower income part of the city

Exito, a modern department store in Los Ejecutivos, an upper middle-income area

An upper middle-income residential neighborhood

The San Pedro neighborhood is another upper-middle income area

PANAMA AS A NATION

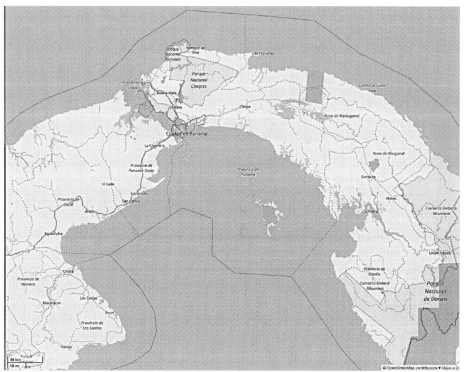

Central Panama (© OpenStreetMap contributors)

The Republic of Panama is a slender nation occupying the isthmus or land bridge between North and South America. The total area of the country is only 75,516 square kilometers or 29,157 square miles and the national population is 4,101,000 people. To which continent does it belong? Prior to the building of the Panama Canal, the traditional boundary between North and South America was at the border between Panama and Colombia. But this is a rather arbitrary political divide that has no real geographic meaning. Once the canal was opened there was a waterway that had to be spanned by bridges, thus it became the recognized boundary between the continents.

Panama is a tropical country, its mountainous spine covered in dense rainforest. The mountains in the west are relatively rugged, but as you traverse the isthmus to the east, the mountains are both lower and less dominating, and that is why the site for the canal was chosen. In the southern margins of the country, serious over cutting of the forest for commercial purposes has exposed much land to erosion and it is not as attractive for settlement. With a humid, tropical climate rainfall occurs on a regular basis, but the two heaviest periods are April through May and October through November. Much of the country is unsettled and still somewhat unspoiled, a potential Panama is trying to exploit through the new concept of ecotourism. The government is attempting to attract visitors who travel to neighboring Costa Rica in hopes of showing off its own rainforest locales. And in the far western high mountains, many American expatriates have found that the climate and environment are much like Costa Rica, thus settling in and around the towns of San Andrés and Boquete.

PANAMA'S HISTORY: As a modern nation, Panama owes its existence to the United States wanting to build a canal across the narrow portion of the lower Central American isthmus. Previous plans to build a canal through Nicaragua were scuttled because of the higher elevations involved combined with a great danger from earthquakes and volcanic eruptions as well as a longer distance through which to dig out a route. At the start of the 20th century when the United States decided upon the present location, Panama was a province of the Republic of Colombia.

The early exploration of Panama dates back to 1513, when Spanish explorer Vasco de Balboa crossed the isthmus and laid eyes on the Pacific. Once Peru and Ecuador were settled, gold and silver were brought by ship up the Pacific coast and then hauled overland to be loaded on ships in the Caribbean to sail across to Spain. Those who settled in Panama exploited the native population, utilizing their forced labor on plantations under what was called the economienda system or in the transport gangs where they were often worked until they dropped.

Dutch, French and British privateers had their eye on Panama and there were raids including the 1671 raid by Englishman Henry Morgan that sacked Panama City, one of the wealthiest cities in Spanish America. But Spain maintained its iron grip until revolutionary fever swept through their colonial empire. In 1821, two independence movements occurred, one in Panama City and the other in Azuero where the farmers of the peninsula were hopeful of independence both from Spain and the government in the capital city of Panama. Through skillful bribery and political maneuvering a crisis was averted and all of Panama declared independence in unison. Knowing their economic weakness and lack of infrastructure, the government of Panama voluntarily joined with Colombia as a province rather than becoming a republic in its own right. But unrest within Panama led to attempts to break away from Colombia in 1831 and between 1899 and 1903.

What was fortunate for the Panamanians was Colombia's rejection of the American bid to build a canal across the isthmus, wanting more money and concessions. Rather than pay Colombia, the United States supported the people of Panama in their bid for independence to which Colombia could do nothing but protest, especially with American war ships off the coast of Panama. Sending troops against the United States was out of the question. Who was president at this time? It was Theodore Roosevelt, known for his diplomatic prowess of speaking softly but carrying a big stick.

THE CANAL ZONE: In the conclusion of a treaty, the United States was granted sovereign rights to a zone 10 miles wide and 50 miles long over which it would have full jurisdiction and fly its own flag. It would be in this zone that the Panama Canal would be dug. Over the years, Panamanians came to resent the presence of a foreign swath of territory bisecting their nation. Agitation continued to fester, as Panama saw its share of dictatorial and military governments, but most of the leadership supported the United States, fearing its military might and welcoming infusions of its money.

In June 1987, retired Colonel Roberto Diaz Herrera openly denounced the regime and exposed its activities. This prompted the Cruzada Civilista to call for massive strikes and demonstrations that would totally destabilize the country. And Noriega's response was swift, leading to mass killings, torture and rape. Order was restored, but the United States hit the government with numerous economic sanctions in 1988, causing the gross domestic product to decline by over 25 percent in a few months. The United States then froze all Panamanian government assets, further crippling the country. In the 1989 elections, the public voted almost en mass for the opposition candidate, but Noriega annulled the results, continuing his repressive rule. And on this basis the United States decided to act.

The United States undertook a bold and controversial move and invaded Panama City in December 1989, to capture Manuel Noriega, the President of Panama. Noriega had become involved with drug cartels and was utilizing his office to funnel drugs through his country into the United States. Panama was also serving as a conduit for illegal migrants from China attempting to smuggle into the United States, a lucrative operation for the Noriega regime. But when one member state of the Pan American Union or the United Nations invades another that is a serious breach of both charters. It is fortunate that Noriega was seen throughout the Americas as a pariah and thus remained relatively silent on the matter. The Panamanian people quickly set about to restore their capital city, parts of which had been badly damaged or destroyed by the Noriega regime to cause added panic. With American economic assistance and advisory aid, Panama has been restored to a level of order with free elections.

Key to economic success was a series of treaties negotiated under the administration of President Jimmy Carter that would allow the Panama Canal to revert to the government of Panama at the end of 1999. Under the terms of the treaty, if the canal should ever come under any military threat, the United States would have the sole right to intervene and protect the infrastructure. In addition, Panama would do nothing to block the rights of all nations to transit the canal. One of the most important provisions of the treaty was that the separate status of the Canal Zone would end in October 1979 as a prelude to all assets being handed over to Panama at the end of 1999, which of course it has. Panama is now in sole control of the canal, but still uses many former Canal Zone personnel because of their expertise.

PANAMA TODAY: The nation of Panama has seen great economic success with one of the lowest unemployment rates of under three percent and a surplus production of basic food for domestic use and export. However, poverty still does exist in the less fortunate mestizo and native communities, the slums of Panama City testimony to the ongoing problem. As much as one quarter of the population lives in a state of poverty with three percent in extreme conditions. Yet overall, Panama is considered to be a second world nation with an overall high standard of living.

The success is due to both the importance of the canal and the great revenue it generates. But given the role of shipping, Panama City has become an important financial hub. The investment of 5.25 billion U. S. Dollars in the building of the new, wider and longer locks will enable more shipping through the canal and generate even greater revenue. This will encourage more financial and trading companies to consider Panama as a hub for operations. Light manufacturing has also become an important factor, utilizing cheaper labor and having access to the canal for global shipping. It is still too early to see just how profitable the new locks will be, but there is every indication from increasing traffic that it is going to be the wisest investment the country could have made.

In the mountainous interior, exploitation of copper and gold will also add to the economic wealth. However, these deposits are located within areas that had been designated as ecological reserves. This riles many factions within the country as well as abroad. And it could impact the growing ecotourism market.

Tourism plays a massive role in the Panamanian economy. Tourism is predicated upon visiting the ecological reserves, viewing the canal and most importantly, buying real estate for second homes or retirement. Special zones have been established where tax exemptions are provided, making either temporary or permanent living quite appealing. Over 2.2 million tourists come to Panama on average each year, and this does not count those who view a slice of the country from the deck of cruise ships. Although they do not spend money in the country, if it were not for Panama Canal cruises, the overall revenue of the country would diminish by the loss of the heavy tolls that cruise ships pay, generally in excess of $100,000 for a single transit.

Panama City has become one of the most spectacular modern cities in Central America, with a population today of 1,501,000 people out of the total 4,101,000 in the entire nation. It has also become the major air hub for Central America with flights arriving and departing for the United States, Canada, the Caribbean, and all major centers in Latin America as well as Europe.

The thick Panamanian rainforest

Tourists on a boat trip down the Rio Pequení

Barú volcano in the western mountain region (Work of Desi burgos, CC BY SA 4.0, Wikimedia.org)

The expatriate town of Boquete in the shadow of Barú volcano (Work of Ayaita, CC BY SA 3.0, Wikimedia.org)

The skyline of Panama City is quite spectacular

Panama City skyline seen from the Panama Canal exit

SAN BLAS ISLANDS

This brief chapter is for the benefit of those more upmarket cruise lines that do make a special stop at one of the San Blas Islands of Panama to allow guests to spend time among the Kuna Indians. This is a very special experience, one that is quite memorable. Unfortunately these small islands cannot accommodate thousands of visitors at any one time, which makes it next to impossible for the larger ships to visit the day before their Panama Canal transit or the day after, depending upon direction of travel.

The San Blas Island archipelago sits off the northeast coast of Panama. The group consists of 335 to 378 very tiny coral islands of which only 49 are inhabited. These are a necklace of low lying, sandy islands that are a mere few feet above the highest storm waves, but fortunately hurricanes do not track into this part of the Caribbean. Many of the islands are so small as to simply have a handful of palm trees and a bit of undergrowth, the proverbial desert island that we see in cartoons or movies where someone is shipwrecked. They have no sources of fresh water, as they are too small to have streams or lakes. Inhabitants must depend upon collecting rainwater in order to survive. These are among several low lying coral islands in the world that are in great danger of disappearing should sea levels continue to rise this century resulting from global warming. But unlike several of the other island groups, the Kuna Indians are citizens of Panama and would therefore benefit by being absorbed even though their homes would be lost.

Until the Spanish came to Panama, the Kuna were one of several tribes inhabiting the northern coast of the isthmus. They lived by hunting and fishing, and had few tools. They also did not practice any farming techniques. The Spanish saw them as essentially sub human and either killed them or drove them off the mainland to the islands where they took refuge and survived.

They were a simple people, wore little or no clothing and painted distinctive geometric designs on their bodies. When Catholic missionaries started to spread across Panama, they were horrified by the Kuna and quickly set about to get them into clothes. So the Kuna began to create their designs out of scraps of colored cloth and sewed them onto their garments. Today what are called "molas" are a popular trade item that represent the artistic nature of the Kuna, an outgrowth from body decoration in pre missionary days.

Over the years, especially into the late 19th and early 20th centuries, some Kuna men ventured to the mainland where they took primarily menial jobs, learning skills that could lead to more than subsistence. A few went to work for the Panama Canal Company when it was still under American ownership, and today they have pensions that enable them to live somewhat above the average, yet most choose to return to their native islands and live a simple life among their own people.

The Kuna women generally remain at home, and on some of the larger islands the children do have government provided primary schools. The women maintain the traditions of the past and engage in the production of craft items, especially molas in the form of dresses and shirts. When cruise ships visit, they dress in their most colorful garb and offer their wares for sale. It is quite a colorful experience to walk among the narrow streets of a Kuna village and see the colorful people. But because of tourism, they have learned to ask for money if you wish to photograph them. I always recommend that you take at least 25 to 30 dollars U. S. funds in single bills so as to be able to pay the one or two dollar fee asked when you wish to take their picture. The women also set up tables along the narrow streets or in the town square and offer their colorful creations for sale.

There are no docking facilities for ships on any of the islands. If your ship is stopping at one of the San Blas Islands, it will anchor a few miles offshore and tenders (lifeboats) will be used to ferry guests to and from the islands. This is an event for the Kuna and they welcome us with open arms. However, they do understand the value of money and price their shirts, dresses and other items at a nominal price that visitors will be willing to pay. Remember that these are all handmade items even though some uses is made of portable sewing machines.

The inhabited islands are not very beautiful, as the Kuna build their wood and thatched houses close together and there are few if any trees left. Outhouses are the only source of waste disposal and they are built at the ends of the piers out over the water, which provides for continuous disposal. But over decades, the surrounding waters do become polluted and on occasion smell rather ripe. There is no rural electricity and the only power available is that generated by individuals or groups, so power is used judiciously.

This is a chance to visit a people who live a third world existence more out of choice today than necessity. As citizens of Panama they are allowed to settle on the mainland, but for centuries these islands have become their home going back to the days when they were not welcome on the mainland. Many of the men do leave to work on the mainland of Panama, and they come to accept modernity, yet when they do return to their families, they come back to a primitive existence.

You will find the people quite friendly. And if you are walking in a small group, you may sometimes be invited into a private home. Please be courteous and do not show your dismay over the conditions under which these people live. It is hard for us to absorb a lifestyle so alien to our own, but being gracious will reward you with a rare opportunity. Normally the Kuna will not offer you anything to eat or drink, as they somehow know that we would prefer to not sample their food. So it is very rare that you will be confronted with the decision - to eat or not to eat.

As noted before, most of the major cruise ships do not stop in the San Blas Islands, so this chapter only applies to such cruise lines as Silversea, Seaborne or Regent. It is not that the larger companies look down upon such a visit; it is just that logistically it would be impossible for thousands of guests from a large ship to be landed on one of these small islands.

The tiny coral islands of San Blas off the coast of Panama

A father and son out on their tiny boat for subsistence fishing

Fishermen docking next to their homes on the tiny islets of San Blas

On tourist ship day all of the houses are decked out with molas for sale

A woman pounding grain for flour to make the daily bread

This is what a two-dollar payment buys in a posed photo

What an incredible picture for a dollar, classic old Kuna costume

Sanitary conditions are rather grim

STRUCTURE OF THE PANAMA CANAL

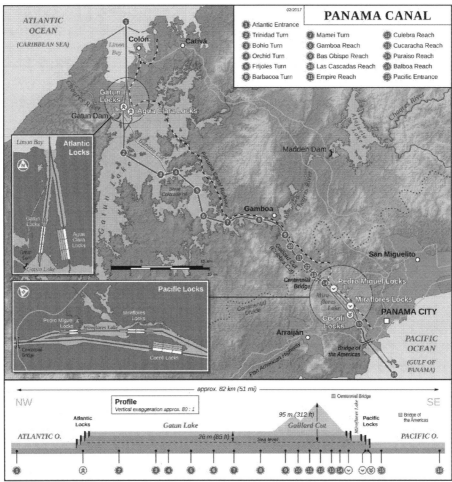

A detailed map of the Panama Canal with diagrams of the locks
and a cross section of the elevations (Work of Thomas Römer,
OpenStreetMap data, CC BY SA 2.0, Wikimedia.org)

A transit through the Panama Canal is a memorable event, most
ship passengers making the journey one time. As the ship is lifted
up through the locks, it is hard at first to appreciate the magnitude
of the operation and the engineering involved. This chapter will
provide you with factual information regarding the scope of the
Panama Canal. And it will preview the new wider locks that went
into service in 2016 to accommodate much longer and wider ships.
In 1914, every ship afloat was able to fit through the locks. But
today in 2018, approximately half of the world's freight carriers, oil
tankers and many of the mega cruise ships are too large to make

the transit even with the new larger locks. So this means the lengthy journey through the Straits of Magellan to transit between the two oceans.

BUILDING THE CANAL: The United States was not the first nation to attempt building a canal across Panama. That honor falls to France, when in 1881, a shareholding company founded by Ferdinand de Lesseps, attempted to dig a sea level canal across the isthmus. Ferdinand de Lesseps was fresh from his success in digging the Suez Canal, a sea level waterway connecting the eastern Mediterranean with the Red Sea, eliminating the long journey around the southern tip of Africa. By 1889, the company was bankrupt and de Lesseps was ruined and disgraced. Miscalculations regarding the geology, the impact of malaria and yellow fever and the primitive nature of the available digging equipment combined to cost the company 22,000 human lives and $US28,000,000. And allegations of corruption ultimately put Charles de Lesseps, the founder's son, in prison for five years.

Assuming they had been successful, what they did not recognize was the great tidal variance between the Caribbean and Pacific sides of the isthmus. Tidal surges of up to 6.7 meters or 22 feet on the Pacific side of the canal would have torn through the sea level canal and made transit so dangerous as to have been impossible. And the erosive power of such a tidal surge would have damaged or destroyed the banks of the canal. And such a surge twice each day would have swept fish and other crustaceans from the Pacific into the Caribbean, altering the natural balance of specie.

In 1894 a second French company was created to continue work on the trans-isthmus railroad and maintain the equipment in working order for hopeful sale to a prospective buyer. In 1904, the United States took over and found that the French equipment and infrastructure had little value because most of it had rusted in the humid tropical climate.

The first two American project directors found it difficult to work within the bounds of the Isthmian Canal Commission, and both resigned before making any progress. President Roosevelt appointed John Frank, the engineer responsible for building the Great Northern Railroad. Frank bypassed all of the bureaucratic structure and ultimately worked directly for the President and

Secretary of War. He set about to first make life comfortable, safe and disease free for the thousands of workers, something the French company had never considered. And Colonel William Goras, chief sanitation officer, was given wide latitude in seeing to it that the living sites remained habitable. It was Dr. Carlos Finlay and Dr. Walter Reed that recognized the spread of yellow fever and malaria came from mosquitos, and spraying was instituted to lessen the danger.

By 1907, Frank had resigned and the final engineer appointed was George Washington Goethals of the Army Crops of Engineers. With his West Point background and strong leadership skills combined with brilliant engineering knowledge, he saw the project through to its ultimate successful fruition. And he very wisely kept in place all of the changes made by William Goras with regard to sanitation and the health of the crew.

After careful geological review, it was decided that a sea level canal would be a disaster because of the strong Pacific tidal range. Thus the American plan was to build a dam to hold back the Chagres River to a depth of 26 meters or 85 feet behind the dam. The river flows north to the Caribbean and often rampaged during the rainy season. The dam was to create Gatun Lake to regulate the flow of the river. This massive man-made lake would flood the lowlands, leaving a chain of islands that today add great beauty to the landscape. Now in the first hundred years, species deviations are starting to be seen among the plant and animal life now cut off on the various islands.

Locks would be built to raise and lower ships through the system. A lock is a large concrete chamber that is flooded with water to equal the sea level where the ship is waiting. The ship sails in and the rear gates close. Then more water is added to raise the ship to the level of the next lock, or water is released to lower it in the case of ships exiting the system. Once the water levels equalize, the front gates are opened and the ship sails up higher in elevation or down, depending on whether it is entering or leaving the canal.

Three massive pairs of locks had to be built to raise and lower ships 26 meters or 85 feet into or out of Gatun Lake. These locks are 33.5 meters or 320 meters or 110 feet wide, and 1,050 feet long. Their height is not equal in every case, but in combination enable the raising or lowering of ships by 26 meters or 85 feet. The walls of the locks are massive in thickness, starting at 14.9 meters or 49 feet at their base and tapering to 2.9 meters or 9.8 feet at the top. The center wall is 17.9 meters or 59 feet thick and rises to accommodate the workstations and two sets of tracks for diesel-electric locomotives that help steer a ship through the canal. There are also tracks along the outer edges of the locks, thus providing for an equalization of the ship within the lock. Ships use minimal power, as the locomotives, called mules, do not pull the ships through. They only keep them straight through the use of thick cables that they can loosen or tighten. All action is coordinated between the mules by a series of bells that you will hear being rung throughout the time the ship is in the locks.

The steel doors at each end of the locks are enormous, varying from 14.3 to 24.9 meters or 47 to 82 feet in height, and they are over seven feet thick. Each gate has two leaves that are 19.8 meters or 65 feet wide, closing to form a V shape. The gates are operated by hydraulic equipment that is water operated, utilizing hydraulic struts installed in 1998. To fill or empty one lock is quite an undertaking, as it involves 101,070,494 liters or 26,700,000 gallons for each use. The water is of course recycled to avoid the massive waste that would otherwise occur, especially during the drier season. It takes only a few minutes to fill or drain the water in the lock to enable the ship to be raised or lowered.

The low mountains that cross the isthmus in the middle had to be breached, as this was also the continental divide. Steam shovels were put to work to cut a channel through the mountains, today known as the magnificent Culebra Cut, which is 12.5 kilometers or 7.8 miles long. This has had the effect of allowing water from the Atlantic side of the isthmus to now channel through to the Pacific side.

Two smaller reservoirs had to be built to regulate water flow for the locks on the Pacific side of the continental divide and to accommodate tidal ranges. The geology of the Pacific side was such that only two pairs of locks could be accomplished on the far end of the Pacific side, with a small man-made reservoir behind the rear lock. Then ships sail a short distance between the two sets of Pacific locks and the single lock at the western end of the Culebra Cut. This is the only lock set that is single.

The maximum size of a ship that can transit the existing locks is referred to as Panamax class. The ship must be capable of fitting into the lock with various minimum limits as to clearance. The height of the ship's tallest mast or funnel must be able to fit under the older Bridge of the Americas at Balboa. And the ship cannot draw more than 12.4 meters or 41.2 feet of water. There will be a new Panamax standard once the parallel new locks are completed. Ships of 25 percent greater length, 51 percent greater width and 26 percent deeper draft will be accommodated. But there will still be a sizable number of ships too large to pass through these new locks. American aircraft carriers, for example, are far too wide on their flight deck to pass through even the new lock structure.

THE ORDER OF PASSAGE: On the Caribbean side a massive breakwater provides protection while ships are waiting to enter the locks. The three Gatun Locks are in tandem and they connect the Caribbean Sea with Gatun Lake. The lake feeds into the Culebra Cut, which then connects with the single Pedro Miguel Lock. The small Miraflores Reservoir connects the Pedro Miguel Lock with the two tandem sets of Miraflores Locks. Balboa Reach then connects the Miraflores Locks with the Pacific Ocean. And there is a long breakwater on the Pacific side to again protect ships from storm surges and normal tidal ranges.

Most people who have made the transit both ways will tell you that entering from the Caribbean Sea is more dramatic because of the three Gatun Locks in tandem. The sight of three ships at different levels of being raised is quite spectacular. At present both sets of the Gatun Locks are used for westbound traffic entering the canal in the morning and then reverse to outbound traffic in the afternoon. This is necessary to accommodate the demand for transit. Without reservations a ship can wait for days to be put into a queue. Cruise ships are always given priority so that passengers can enjoy maximum daylight.

Entering from the Pacific side and traveling eastbound is still dramatic, but there are only the two Miraflores Locks visible as the ship enters the system. Both sets of locks are also used for inbound traffic in the morning, and ships then pass one another in the Culebra Cut and Gatun Lake as they head for their respective exits.

The Pedro Miguel Lock is separated by over a mile in distance. And it is a single lock system with both locks used for one-way traffic. Thus many feel that this entry from the Pacific is not quite as dramatic. I have done the transit both ways several times and frankly find each to be exciting. The reason for the Pacific side having this different configuration is based upon the geology. The rock layers are not as strong in any significant block wide enough to accommodate three locks in tandem.

It should be noted that even though the terms eastbound and westbound are used in reference to crossing the isthmus. The orientation of the canal is from northwest to southeast. This means that the Caribbean side is several miles farther west in longitude than the Pacific side. And in actual transit, ships are traveling on a northwest-southeast axis. But with total agreement that the Pacific Ocean is west of the Atlantic, the journey is thought of as east west or west to east. Quiz programs such as Jeopardy often ask, "Which side of the Panama Canal is farther west, the Atlantic or Pacific?" And of course most people will say the Pacific side.

With the new locks inaugurated in 2016, there is now quite an increase in traffic, as both sets of locks are operating simultaneously/ The Culebra Cut had to be widened to accommodate the potential demand. The new locks are 426.7 meters or 1,400 feet long and 54.8 meters or 180 feet wide and 126.8 centimeters or 60 feet deep. The locks raise or lower ships the full amount on the Pacific side in one set of locks unlike the present Miraflores and Pedro Miguel Lock configuration of three locks.

French engineer Ferdinand de Lesseps portrayed in the media

Building the great canal locks

Digging the Culebra Cut with primitive steam shovels

The USS Ancon, the first ship to transit the canal in 1914

TRAVERSING THE CANAL
EAST TO WEST

At present, the majority of cruise ships passing through the Panama Canal are utilizing the old lock system. The new locks at present are more limited with regard to the number of cruise ships they will accept, as their primary focus is on the heavy bulk carriers and container ships. Thus these next two chapters describe passage through the lock system that has been in use since the opening of the canal. From the point of view of giving passengers the greatest spectacle, the older locks herein described are far more elegant in their operation than the new locks, which although being ultra modern, lack the power to impress like the older existing locks.

Normally at dawn your ship will be entering the breakwater at the eastern or Caribbean entrance to the Panama Canal. As the sun rises, you will see many cargo ships or tankers dotting the horizon, anchored and awaiting their turn to travel westbound through the canal. Tolls are lower for unreserved travel, and generally the smaller and less affluent shipping companies simply wait and take their chances that they will be able to transit within a few days. The major shipping lines and all cruise ships line up in the order they are given to begin the approximately one hour transit through the three contiguous Gatun Locks.

Generally cruise ships are placed at or close to the head of the line. The Panama Canal Company recognizes the value of good public relations that will be spread by the thousands of cruise ship passengers who have a memorable transit. To further facilitate good relations, when the motor launch approaches from the Caribbean port of Colon, it carries not only the pilot who will serve on the bridge to coordinate the transit, but also a special guide who will narrate the transit over the course of the day. As a Destination Consultant for Silversea Cruises, and having made the transit numerous times, I have had the great privilege of narrating the transit along with the Panamanian guide. And guest has found it quite rewarding to hear a dialogue between two narrators.

The majority of passengers will be forward on the upper decks for the best view of the entry into the lower of the three Gatun Locks. Given that both sets are used for westbound traffic in the morning, the ship may be assigned to either the left or right side lock. Slowly the ship will sail alongside the middle wall, almost inching its way forward. Then when it is close enough to where the cables can be attached from the diesel-electric locomotives, henceforth called mules, waiting on either side, men in small boats come out to bring the lines close enough where ship's crew can reach down with a hook and bring them on board to be attached to one of the winches. Once the ship is fully attached to two mules forward and two aft, the ship slowly sails into the lock and then stops. Behind the ship, the massive steel doors will close. And within moments water begins to flood upward from the many openings in the bottom of the lock. It takes less than ten minutes for the millions of gallons needed to flood in and raise the ship to the level where it will be equalized with the middle lock. With a ringing of various bells, the mules coordinate their positions while the forward lock doors slowly rotate open. And now ahead of the ship is the middle lock into which the ship slowly sails while being kept in a straight path by the tightening or loosening of the steel cables by the mules.

Once in the middle lock, the process is repeated. The rear gates, which are much taller than those in the first lock chamber, close and soon the water level begins to rise, as millions of gallons flood into the lock. And within a few minutes, the forward doors will rotate open and the third lock becomes visible. One again the mules coordinate their guidance while the ship slowly sails into the uppermost of the Gatun Locks. Once in the upper lock, the process repeats itself for a third and final time. The rear gates close, the lock fills and at last the ship is raised to a height of 85 feet above sea level. But now when the forward gates rotate open, ahead of the ship is the first look at the northern end of Gatun Lake, a blue gem surrounded by lush, verdant hills cloaked in tropical rainforest and dotted with many islands that are the remnants of hilltops not drowned with the lake formed. As the ship sails into Gatun Lake, you will notice on the right hand (starboard) side the back of the curved structure of Gatun Dam, the cornerstone that holds the entire canal system together by regulating the waters of the Chagres River that it holds back as Gatun Lake.

During your transit through the Gatun Locks you may have caught glimpses of the new channel being cut for the wider and longer locks to accommodate larger vessels. This construction is taking place off of the port side of the ship, but it is difficult to catch a clear view of the work being done.

Now your ship is in the widest part of Gatun Lake, several miles across in all directions. The speed limit for crossing the lake is relatively slow, around 10 knots per hour, making for a leisurely sailing. If the weather is nice, the richness of the surrounding rainforest is quite striking set against the deep blue of the lake and a sky normally dotted with cumulus clouds. And by late morning, if there will be any rain, you can see thunderheads massing along the continental divide.

Looking at the detailed map at the end of this chapter, you will notice that the route for ship traffic crosses the broad expanse of the lake where several tributary streams come together to have created a flat valley that flooded to create the lake. But the traffic route continues across at an angle heading up the now flooded main channel of the Chagres River. The large Barro Colorado Island helps to narrow the main channel to less than a mile in width. But now sailing into these narrower waters, you have a chance to come close enough to the rainforest that even without the aid of binoculars you will see monkeys in the trees, get an occasional sighting of colorful birds and along the shores of the lake you will see Cayman, the larger version of the alligator. Depending upon the heat factor, often the Cayman are lazing along the banks or you may even see them swimming in the margins of the river. The on board guide will generally point them out. Barro Colorado Island is home to the Smithsonian Tropical Research Institute and is therefore a protected reserve.

An important sight is the town of Gamboa, about three to four hours sailing time from when first entering the Gatun Locks. Gamboa is an important maintenance center, but its origin dates to the digging of the Culuebra Cut. Today Gamboa is home to the Panama Canal Dredging Division. The town is located where the Chagres River makes a sharp turn to the south, and at this point your ship will be entering the totally man-made channel that becomes the Culebra Cut and penetrates the low mountains ahead. The bridges crossing the river carries both highway and railway traffic between Colon and Panama City. And if you are fortunate enough, you may see the passenger train that makes the journey several times a day. When a cruise ship is approaching, the engineer often stops the train for its passengers to enjoy watching the ship pass, and of course this enables you to get some good pictures of the train.

Gamboa today is only a shadow of what it was during the digging of the Culebra Cut. Today only a handful of families live here, but there are many fine examples of the residential architecture, mostly wood, that characterized the American adaptation to this hot, tropical landscape. But the highlight is seeing one or two of the massive dredges in their docking facility at Gamboa. The large red and white crane that you will see tied up in the docking area is used when it is necessary to change one of the massive steel gates in the lock system. It is one of the largest cranes of its kind in the world. The dredges are used to keep the upper end of the lake, which is actually the Chagres River and also the Culebra Cut at its new depth of 60 feet to enable the deepest draft vessels passage unhindered. Small slides from the walls of the cut and debris washed down by heavy summer rains can cause a build up that needs to constantly be dredged to keep the entire waterway open.

After leaving Gamboa, your ship will enter the Culebra Cut, a 12.5 kilometer or 7.8-mile channel that was dug through the Continental Divide where hills rather than mountains only rise to heights of less than 305 meter or 1,000 feet. But it was still difficult to blast and dig with the types of steam shovels that existed at the time to create a channel capable of maintaining a draft deep enough for ships. Fortunately the Americans recognized that digging all the way to sea level was not necessary, as a direct ocean-to-ocean contact would have been disastrous because of the Pacific tidal range. That extra depth would have been a significant undertaking ending in disaster.

The Culebra Cut is spectacular when you consider that the steep walls had to be carved out of previously existing hills that were cloaked in thick, tropical vegetation. You will notice that the walls are terraced and in many areas there are concrete or wire bracings. This is because of the loose nature of the rock layers and the potential for minor earthquakes both factors that would cause small landslides and clog the channel. Widening of the channel took place over the past few years, but you will see some cutting and dredging operations at work. This is necessary to maintain the slightly wider channel to accommodate the larger ships are passing through the Culebra Cut now that the new locks are completed.

The ship will pass under a new and quite beautiful suspension bridge, known today as the Centennial Bridge, built to carry the Pan American Highway across the canal, connecting both sides of Panama with a modern highway. It was opened to correspond with the first century of Panamanian independence. The bridge now carries the bulk of the traffic between the two halves of the country. Just beyond the bridge, on the starboard side of the ship you will see the merging of the new channel that now carries larger ships from the new locks on the Pacific side into the Culebra Cut. With the new sets of locks, overall traffic through the canal has increased, necessitating greater care in keeping ships separated and operations at a safe level.

The Culebra Cut ends with the single Pedro Miguel Lock set. Your ship will once again enter either the left or right lock, but first it will slow down while coming alongside the long center divider strip. Approaching any of the locks from above as part of the sailing out process appears to be far less spectacular. As you look ahead at the lock, all you see is the already filled lock basin, which is at the same level of the ship. You do not get to appreciate the height and mass of the lock gates because they are mainly under the water. As they rotate open to enable your ship to sail into the lock, the drama does not appear to be the same as when the ship was passing into the canal. But the actual operation is truly as dramatic as when inbound. Only the visual perception is lacking.

The ship will come to a stop to again have the cables brought out by small boat and grabbed by operational personnel who will attach them to the ships winch system. The mules will align the ship in the center of the channel and it will sail slowly into the single lock. As the rear lock gates close, water will begin to in this case drain from the lock since now the ship is in the process of being lowered to the level of Miraflores Lake, which is 9.4 meters or 31 feet lower than the 25.9 meter or 85 foot level the ship has been at since passing out of the Gatun Locks. The process will take about 10 to 15 minutes, and then the forward lock gates will rotate open to allow the ship to sail into the small man-made Miraflores Lake.

A small dam was placed across the Pedro Miguel River to create Miraflores Lake, filling a basin dredged deep enough to enable ships to connect between the Culebra Cut and Pacific Ocean. The transit across the lake is 1.9 kilometers or 1.2 miles and then the long central strip of the Miraflores Locks will come into view. And once again there is a lessened sense of drama because the upper lock into which your ship will sail is already filled to the same level as Miraflores Lake.

The process of slowing to a stop to have the steel cables link the ship to the four mules takes place and then the ship slowly sails into the upper Miraflores lock to await being lowered to the final lock that will ultimately place the ship at sea level. The final drop is 16.4 meters or 54 vertical feet accomplished with the two-stage lock system. The reason for the separation of the Pedro Miguel Lock was the inability of the surrounding geological structure to accommodate three locks operating in tandem as was seen on the Caribbean side.

The Miraflores Lock Visitor's Center is a popular attraction for both tourists to Panama City and passengers on board ship. As your ship enters the upper of the two Miraflores locks and is positioned in front of the forward gates, you will be face to face on the port side with the four levels of the visitor's center. Normally on a nice day the balconies are thronged with tourists who come to watch ships pass through the canal. In the morning hours they watch ships being raised into Miraflores Lake. But in the afternoon, by the time your ship has made most of the transit, visitors will be awaiting the arrival of outbound cruise ships in particular. Notices are posted as to which ships are expected to transit westbound. Visitors will start to waive and cheer, and most captains will blow the ship's main whistle in salute to the visitor's center. And of course passengers will be waiving back to those onshore. It is a celebration of the Panama Canal that occurs every time a cruise ship passes, and something parties both onshore and on board look forward to. Then as both parties are waiving at one another, the forward gates rotate open and the ship is now ready to enter the final lock that will take it down to sea level and the Balboa Reach, the estuary that ultimately leads to the sea in roughly five miles.

As the ship transits through the final lock at Miraflores, you will notice a large development of buildings on the port side horizon. What look like old early 20th century military barracks and government headquarters are the remains of Fort Clayton, once the center of command for the United States Army in charge of security for the Canal Zone. Today the massive facility is used in part for residential purposes, mixed business and educational services, part of it being known as Ciudad de Saber, city of knowledge. It is a collection of academic institutions brought together by a foundation of the same name as the complex.

The final leg of the journey is still very interesting despite being beyond the locks. As the ship enters Balboa Reach, you will have excellent skyline views of Panama City. The ship will pass by a small pleasure craft anchorage and the container cargo terminal for Panama City. The final important structure is the Bridge of the Americas, the original bridge across the canal that once carried the Pan American Highway. Today it carries local traffic.

Beyond the bridge is the very long breakwater protecting Balboa Reach from storm or tidal surges. As the ship starts to gain a bit of speed, the pilot boat will come alongside to take the pilot and guide back to shore. Now the ship is free to navigate out to sea, having made the westbound transit through the Panama Canal. But your memories of this transit will linger with you for years to come.

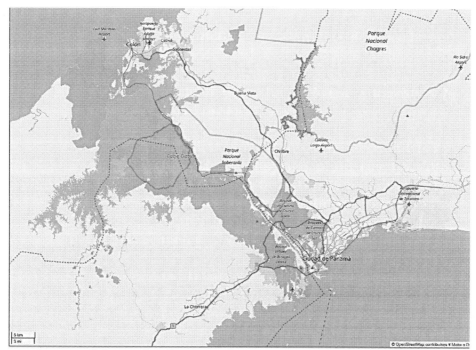

A map of the entire Panama Canal route (© OpenStreetMap contributors)

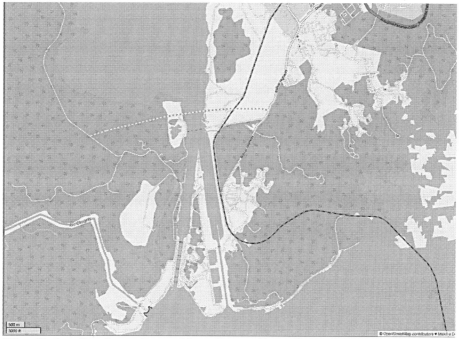

The Gatun Lock system- old and new OpenStreetMapcontributors)

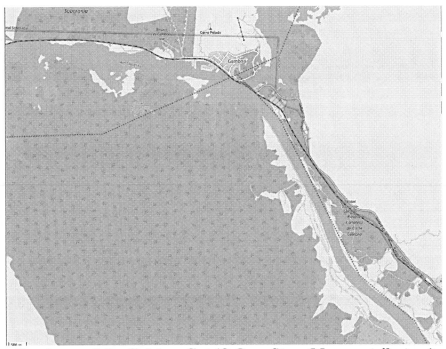

Gamboa and the Culebra Cut (© OpenStreetMap contributors)

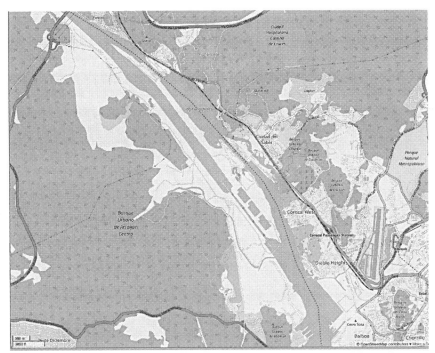

**The Pedro Miguel and Miraflores Lock systems - old and new
(© OpenStreetMap contributors)**

Entering Gatun Lock One from the Caribbean

Entering Gatun Lock number two

One of the mules guiding the ship into Gatun Lock Three

The shoreline of Barro Colorado Island in Gatun Lake

One of the major cranes used to repair the locks, sitting at Gamboa

Dredging at work entering the Culebra Cut

Two way traffic in the Culebra Cut as both entries pass en route outbound

Looking back to Centennial Bridge in the Culebra Cut

Entering the Pedro Miguel Lock heading to the Pacific

In the Pedro Miguel Lock ready to enter Miraflores Lake

About to leave the Miraflores Locks for the Balboa Reach

Cheering crowds at the Miraflores Visitor's Center

The skyline of Panama City from Balboa Reach

Bridge of the Americas and beyond the Pacific Ocean

TRAVERSING THE CANAL
WEST TO EAST

Now we take a virtual journey through the Panama Canal, but this time from the Pacific side eastbound to the Caribbean side using the old lock system, which the majority of cruise ships will continue to use. The entire picture changes, as each transit direction carries its own imagery and sense of wonder. After making several transits in both directions, I personally favor the east to west crossing of the isthmus simply because there is a greater sense of drama when seeing the three Gatun Locks upon entry. Although I must admit that seeing them in the afternoon, as the ship is slowly lowered through each of the three locks is also a dynamic sight.

It is early morning, just as the first light of day is setting the eastern horizon aglow, the ship is passing the long breakwater on the Pacific side of the Panama Canal. This breakwater, several miles in length, helps protect the estuary known as Balboa Reach from extreme storm surges or tidal ranges. On the Pacific side, the tidal range can be as high as 6.7 22 feet whereas on the Caribbean side it averages three to four feet. And storm surges are extremely rare.

As the ship slowly inches along the breakwater, the twinkling lights of Panama City's massive line of beachfront skyscrapers slowly wink out with the coming dawn. Soon the pilot boat brings both the pilot who will guide the ship and a Panamanian guest guide who will provide a running commentary while the ship passes through the canal. I have had the great pleasure of working right along with the Panamanian guide to provide a joint commentary from the bridge while the ship is making the crossing both on the eastbound and westbound transits. And I always find it quite a thrilling experience to be able to share my observations with the passengers.

The ship passes under the Bridge of the Americas, the first bridge across the canal that once carried the Pan American Highway, lining the country together. But today a modern suspension bridge farther inland is the main national link. After passing under the old steel bridge, you will get a glimpse of the Panama City skyline and the cargo container terminal, both on the ship's starboard side.

Approaching the two sets of Miraflores Locks for anyone on their first crossing is quite a sight. As the ship reaches the outermost center strip, men in small boats will bring out the lines for the port side diesel-electric locomotives, henceforth called by their proper name of mules. There will be two mules on each side of the ship, not pulling the ship through the locks, but keeping it steady by loosening or tightening the steel cables, as the ship navigates on minimal power. Most passengers come with the notion from documentary films that the mules actually pull the ship through. By the use of a series of ringing bells, the mules communicate from one side of the lock to the other as to which ropes need to be loosened or tightened to keep the ship in mid channel. Hearing the ringing of the bells is a part of the total experience of transiting the canal. Depending upon which lock the ship will use, right or left side, determines which lines are attached first. The center wall carries tracks for the mules operating on both locks. Initially two-way traffic was the norm, but as use of the canal has increased, today only one-way traffic is permitted during the day. Traffic proceeds through both sets of locks inbound on both sides until around noon. Then outbound traffic is permitted only on both sides, clearing the entire system by evening. At night two-way traffic is permitted, as volume is far lower than during the day.

The Miraflores locks will raise the ship 16.4 meters or 54 vertical feet above sea level in two stages. The ship will enter the first lock at sea level and the rear gates will rotate shut. Then within ten minutes 26,000,000 gallons of water will flood into the lock from below, raising the ship 8.2 meters or 27 feet in elevation. At this point the forward gates will rotate open and the ship will sail into the second lock, guided carefully by the four mules. And the process will begin again with the rear gates closing, the lock flooding and the forward gates opening after the ship has been raised another 8.2 meters or 27 feet. But here at the second Miraflores Lock, on the starboard side you will see a four level tan building with broad open balconies. This is the Miraflores Visitor's Center where cheering crowds wait for ships to enter the locks in the morning or descend in the afternoon. And a cruise ship with its hundreds or thousands of guests lining the upper and forward decks is what they wait for. There is a lot of cheering and waiving of hands along with snapping of photographs on both sides. And normally the captain will please those onshore by blowing the ship's whistle in salute to the crowd. I often wonder if it is just enjoyment at watching the ship entering or exiting the lock, or is it also a bit of envy from those onshore regarding those of us fortunate enough to be on board and making the crossing?

After approximately 45-minutes, the ship will exit the Miraflores Locks and transit the 1.9 kilometers or 1.2 miles of Miraflores Lake. This lake was created by the building of a small dam on the Pedro Miguel River to create sufficient depth and regulate the flow so as to enable ships to continue on into the man-made Culebra Cut. But it is first necessary to transit one further lock to be raised an additional 9.4 meters or 31 feet in elevation. The Culebra Cut, Chagres River and Gatun Lake are all at 25.9 meters or 85 feet above sea level. Three locks were deemed necessary; however, the geological structure of the hills on the Pacific side was such that three consecutive locks were not feasible. There was not enough anchorage for a third lock and small fault lines made any such attempt dangerous. Thus the Pedro Miguel lock set is the only single pair on the entire canal.

As the ship reaches the outermost forward edge of the center strip, once again men in a small boat bring the lines out so that ship's personnel can lower a hook and pull the lines up to the winch. This procedure also takes place on the starboard side. But depending upon whether the ship uses the right or left lock determines which side is first. To transit the Pedro Miguel Lock system it takes the ship approximately half an hour to 40-minutes. On the new locks being built to the northwest of the present Miraflores and Pedro Miguel Locks, all of the locks will be in tandem, as sufficient anchorage was found. These new locks will be much longer and wider, but still will not be able to accommodate the largest ships. The Suez Canal has no locks and is wide enough that it can accommodate any ship presently afloat. It is a true sea level canal that does not even have any surge protector gates as does the Kiel Canal between the North Sea and Baltic Sea.

As the ship leaves the lock, it is now 25.9 meters or 85 feet above sea level and ready to enter the man made Culebra Cut. The cut was dug with steam-powered shovels after sections were first blasted with dynamite. The cut is 12.5 kilometers or7.8-miles in length and crosses the Continental Divide. Here in the middle of Panama, the tall mountains that form the main spine of the country are less than 305 meter or 1,000 feet high. They are essentially hills, thus making it easier to dig a channel to connect both drainage divides. But the layers of rock are not well consolidated, thus the slopes had to grade gently away from the canal and by terracing, using concrete retaining walls and wire mesh, they have been deemed stable. Occasional minor slippages or slides do dump debris into the Culebra Cut, so dredging is an ongoing process. The Culebra Cut is presently being widened to accommodate the larger ships that will start to pass through the new locks as early as Spring 2016.

As you sail through the Culebra Cut, you will soon pass under the Centennial Bridge, a new suspension span that carries the main Pan American Highway across the canal, connecting both halves of Panama that are bisected by the waterway. The bridge was opened in 2004 to commemorate one century of Panamanian independence from Colombia.

Then as you leave the cut after about another hour of sailing, the ship will sail into the Chagres River's middle channel that has been flooded to a stable depth of around 15.2 meter or 50 feet by the Gatun Dam. The river meets the man made channel from the south, which when sailing eastbound is the ship's starboard side. You will see a highway and railway bridge spanning the river just slightly beyond where it meets the cut. And if you are fortunate you may see one of the morning passenger trains that travel between Panama City and Colon. Generally the engineer will stop the train so passengers can enjoy the view of a passing cruise ship, and of course you also have the advantage of seeing one of Panama's nice passenger trains.

The town up ahead along the south bank is Gamboa. Today Gamboa is home only to the Panama Canal Dredging Division. Gamboa is only a shadow of what it was during the digging of the Culebra Cut. Today only a handful of families live here, but there are many fine examples of the residential architecture, mostly wood, that characterized the American adaptation to this hot, tropical landscape. But the highlight is seeing one or two of the massive dredges in their docking facility at Gamboa. The large red and white crane that you will see tied up in the docking area is used when it is necessary to change one of the massive steel gates in the lock system. It is one of the largest cranes of its kind in the world. The dredges are used to keep the upper end of the lake, which is actually the Chagres River and also the Culebra Cut at a depth of over 15.2 meter or 50 feet to enable the deepest draft vessels passage unhindered. Small slides from the walls of the cut and debris washed down by heavy summer rains can cause a build up that needs to constantly be dredged to keep the entire waterway open. With the new locks the depth will be increased to 60 feet for added clearance of the larger vessels.

After leaving Gamboa, you will continue sailing through the relatively narrow channel of the river until you reach the main body of Gatun Lake. Looking at the detailed map at the end of the chapter on the structure of the canal, you will notice that the route for ship traffic will follow the Chagres River, now flooded by Gatun Dam, down to where you will enter the main body of Gatun Lake. The large Barro Colorado Island helps to narrow the main channel to less than a mile in width. But now sailing through these narrower waters before entering the broader lake, you have a chance to come close enough to the rainforest that even without the aid of binoculars you will see monkeys in the trees, get an occasional sighting of colorful birds and along the shores of the lake you will see Cayman, the larger version of the alligator. Depending upon the heat factor, often the Cayman are lazing along the banks or you may even see them swimming in the margins of the river. The on board guide will generally point them out. Barro Colorado Island is home to the Smithsonian Tropical Research Institute and is therefore a protected reserve.

It is through these waters that you will see traffic moving toward the Pacific side of the isthmus. Remember that groups of ships entered from each side in the early morning hours, and now by early afternoon, traffic in both directions passes, each group of ships heading for its respective exit. It is interesting to note the country of registry for the various ships you pass. Always look to the aft end of a container ship or tanker to see its flag of registry. And written across the stern is the name of the ship and its homeport. Two of the most popular for registration of ships to keep taxes low and worker regulations at a minimum are Panama and Liberia. So if the name on the stern is Monrovia that is the capital and main port for Liberia. Among German ships most will be from Hamburg. And you may see several Chinese or Japanese vessels with port names such as Shanghai, Osaka or Yokohama. And ships with Singapore registry are also quite common. Most cruise ships are either registered in the Bahamas, with Nassau as the main port, or they may be registered in Bermuda with Hamilton as the port. Some European ships are registered in Malta and the port on the stern will be Valletta.

When your ship enters the heart of Gatun Lake, you will be on the final leg of your transit across Panama. It will take about an hour or less to cross the width of the lake and by looking either to port or starboard you will see the greater dimension of this man made body of water that is quite impressive. You will also notice many small container ships or tankers anchored around the lake. These are ships belonging to smaller shipping companies that have been transiting the canal without a prior reservation. So they will anchor and wait until they are given a slot to pass through the triple set of the Gatun Locks and out into the Caribbean Sea. As a cruise ship, however, your vessel will sail right to the locks for immediate descent back to sea level.

The three pair of Gatun Locks is the crown jewel of the Panama Canal. Here the underlying geologic structure allowed for the locks to be built in one massive unit. I still find that the most impressive view is had when entering the Gatun Locks and seeing ships in the middle and upper locks with a total elevation difference of 25.9 meter or 85 feet. But once your ship has made the full descent, you can go to one of the aft decks and get pictures of the full height and grandeur of the locks. But even during the descent, you will find these locks to be impressive, especially if there are ships ahead of you. When your ship is in the upper lock and you look down to ships in the middle and lower locks, you still get the full impact of the enormity of the descent.

Once again the procedure is the same as during entry. The ship will sail up to the edge of the middle wall and have the lines brought out by small boat for crew to hook and pull on board to attach to the ship's winches. Then the ship will advance slightly to have the outer lines brought on board, either starboard or portside depending upon which lock set it is assigned to. Once the mules adjust the cables to keep the ship in mid channel, it will slowly sail into the uppermost lock. Only this time after the rear gates close, the water will drain out, lowering the ship approximately 28 feet in elevation to begin the descent to sea level. Once the proper level is reached, the forward gates will rotate open and the ship will sail into the middle lock where the process will be repeated, lowering the ship approximately another 8.5 meters or 28 feet.

As you watch the ship being lowered through the locks, it is also interesting to keep your eye on any ships ahead of yours or in the adjacent lock set. On some occasions where there is a very large container ship that only has a couple feet of clearance on its port and starboard sides, the mules find it difficult to keep the ship perfectly centered. If this happens, the ship will end up scraping one side of the lock and it will send up a cloud of pulverized concrete. The locks do sustain some damage on a recurring basis. These largest of Panamax ships barely squeeze into the locks, and this makes their transit quite tenuous.

After the forward gates rotate open, your ship will sail into the lowermost of the three Gatun Locks. Again the rear gates will close and the water level will be lowered, but this time to sea level. When the forward gates rotate open, the ship will sail forward, stop outside of the lock and have the cables removed. At this point, it has completed its transit through the Panama Canal. All that is needed now is for the ship to sail between the marker buoys to the breakwater where the pilot boat will be waiting to take the pilot and guide off of the ship. Now the ship is free to resume its normal speed and sail out into Caribbean waters, ready to continue on to its next port of call. As you look back at the towering Gatun Locks, you will be reminded of your transit through the canal.

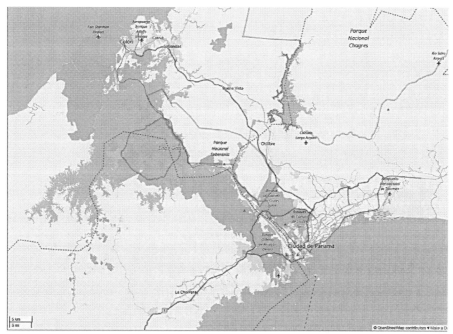

A map of the entire Panama Canal route (© OpenStreetMap contributors)

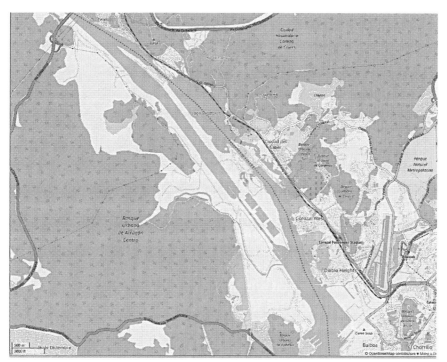

The Pedro Miguel and Miraflores Lock systems - old and new (© OpenStreetMap contributors)

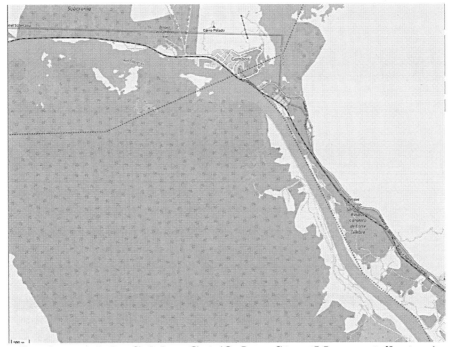

Gamboa and the Culebra Cut (© OpenStreetMap contributors)

The Gatun Lock system- old and new OpenStreetMapcontributors)

Entering the upper Miraflores Lock from the lower lock upon entering the canal

The forward port side mule guiding the ship into the upper Miraflores Lock

A huge container ship enters the adjacent lock

A large container ship barely fits into Miraflores Lock number two

The rich tropical vegetation along the shore of Miraflores Lake

Approaching the Pedro Miguel Lock after crossing Miraflores Lake

About to enter the single Pedro Miguel Lock

The Centennial Bridge crosses at the start of the Culebra Cut

One of the dredges keeping the Culebra Cut free of debris

**The operations center at Gamboa during an afternoon
thundershower**

Crossing Gatun Lake en route to the Gatun Locks

Sailing from the upper to the middle Gatun Lock on the descent

Following a massive container ship from the first to the second Gatun Lock

Watching a large container vessel hit the outside wall of the lower Gatun Lock on the descent

About to be lowered to sea level in the lower Gatun Lock

THE NEW LOCK SYSTEM

On June 26, 2016, the Panama Canal Authority opened the new lock system to traffic after several years of work, including delays. It had been hoped that the new locks could be opened for the 100th anniversary of the opening of the original canal, but unfortunately delays did occur. This new lock system will double the volume of traffic through the canal by allowing for larger ships to pass that previously could not negotiate the older locks. The project entailed building two new sets of locks along with excavating channels that would link into the existing Culebra Cut and Gatun Lake portion of the canal. The locks on the Atlantic side are called the Agua Clara Locks consisting of three chambers, and they are located just to the east of the Gatun Locks and feed into Gatun Lake. On the Pacific side, the new Cocoli Locks consist of three chambers, and they are located to the west of the Miraflores Locks. In addition to the construction of the new locks, the Culebra Cut had to be widened and dredged to a greater depth and the depth of Gatun Lake had to be increased. The government of Panama put the construction of these new locks up to a national referendum in 2006, which passed with 76.8 percent favorable vote. The estimated cost in U. S. dollars was expected to be 5.25 billion, but a final accounting does not appear to be available. The added tolls for the larger ships that will use these new locks should pay for the cost of construction within a reasonable time frame given the estimated total revenue of over U. S. 6 billion dollars annually.

As a result of the larger ships that would be capable of utilizing the new locks, ports along the Atlantic Coast of the United States and as far away as the United Kingdom had to prepare to be capable of receiving these larger ships that previously could not be accommodated. With the demand for greater international trade by sea, the new locks will boost the overall trade between the Asian ports where many goods are produced and those of the Atlantic Coast of the United States and Canada along with those of Western Europe.

Apart from creating a new Panamax size capability, the new locks will also enable the overall canal system to provide better service. With the old locks at capacity, there were several factors that actually were starting to limit the volume of traffic and the transit times. Modern old Panamax size vessels were at a size where they had very little clearance inside the locks. I have even witnessed one large container ship scraping the walls of the Gatun Locks on the way to the Atlantic. Huge clouds of powdered concrete were thrown into the air, as the mules attempted to keep this huge vessel centered in the middle Gatun Lock, but with little success. The pilot on board the Silver Shadow told me that this was a regular occurrence and that it then required repairs to the walls of the lock. With such large ships traversing the locks, overall transit speed had to be reduced and a transit could take over eight hours. The lock mechanisms, although amazing, are over a century old and require a large amount of down time for maintenance, which of course then greatly reduces the volume of traffic, and adds to the overall transit time. Thus the new lock system was a vital necessity for the handling of increasing demand.

The old Panamax size was based upon the capacity of the locks, which are 33.53 meters or 110 feet wide, 320.04 meters or 1,050 feet in length and permitted a draught of 12.56 meters 0r 41.2 feet. Two bridges cross the canal and they set the height limit of 57.91 meters or 190 feet. This was excluding more than 2/3 of present day shipping, including many of the large mega cruise ships. The new Panamax size is now 54.86 meters or 180 feet wide, 426.72 meters or 1,400 feet in length with a maximum draught of 18.29 meters or 60 feet. The height remains the same because of the need to transit under the Centennial Bridge over the Culebra Cut.

Now that the new locks have been successfully opened, many of the intermediate mega cruise ships will be capable of making the transit of the Panama Canal, but at present there are limitations as to how many are being allowed to pass and thus the wait for scheduling is quite long. The first large cruise ship to pass through the new locks was the Disney Wonder, an 83,000 ton ship that passed through in May 2016. Most cruise lines that have mega size ships capable of passing through the new locks are planning to only use them on repositioning cruises when they finish the Caribbean season and relocate the ships to Alaska for the summer or in reverse during the fall. But many of the truly mega ships are still too large to utilize even these larger locks. But for a traditional Panama Canal cruise where the passage is the real heart of the voyage, it will be the smaller and medium size ships that will still continue to ply the older lock system. And frankly, as one who has made the passage four times and had the privilege of broadcasting a live narration, I think that the true essence of a Panama Canal crossing is when it is through the older locks.

If you are planning a cruise that will include the Panama Canal, check the dimensions of your cruise ship, and if it exceeds the old Panamax limit, but the canal is part of the itinerary, then you will have the distinct pleasure of transiting the Panama Canal through the new locks. Perhaps I am a traditionalist, but I would prefer to continue to make the crossing through the canal using the old locks simply because of the history that they represent. There is certain majesty in looking at functioning machinery that is operating in its second century with such a great degree of precision. Of course there have been upgrades to various components such as the steel gates and the electric mules. But the hydraulic system is still functioning as designed.

The new lock system will be far more efficient in its recirculation and use of water, saving many millions of gallons of water. And the new locks operate much more efficiently since they slide horizontally rather than opening on a swing mechanism similar to door. Progress is a wonderful thing to see, but there is also much to say for nostalgia when it comes to the Panama Canal.

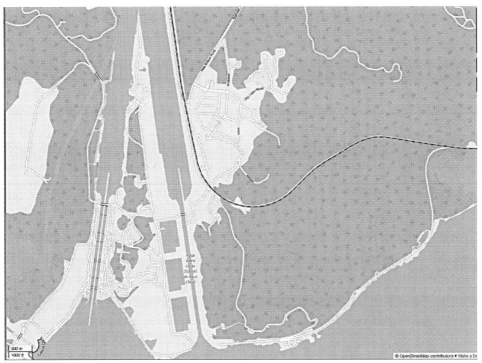

The new locks on the Atlantic side (© OpenStreetMap contributors)

The new locks on the Pacific side (© OpenStreetMap contributors)

Building the sliding gates for the new Panama Canal locks on the Caribbean side (Work of andreu, CC BY SA 3.0, Wikimedia.org)

COLÓN

Colón is the Caribbean port city at the gateway to the Panama Canal. It is also the second largest city in Panama with a metropolitan population of 241,000 residents. Few cruise ships make a port call at Colón, but this chapter is included for the benefit of any reader who may book a cruise with a line that does include this stop. I frankly do not see the value in such a stop because the city has deteriorated since the 1980's. Today Colón's unemployment rate is near 40 percent. It has developed massive barrios with a poverty rate of around 50 percent. And drug addition has been rampant, leading to a significant problem of street crime. Unfortunately the government in Panama City appears to be ignoring the problem, thus while Panama City is vibrant and booming, Colón has lost most of the charm and enticement it once had.

HISTORY: The city owes its founding to American interests in the building of the Panama Railroad, which ran its first passenger train in 1855. The primary motivation was to shorten the distance to the California gold fields. One could take a ship from an east coast port to Colón, then take the short 76.6 kilometer or 47.6-mile railroad journey to Balboa and board a ship to San Francisco. This cut a couple months of sailing around the bottom of South America through the Straits of Magellan.

During the period before the Panama Canal, the railroad carried both passengers and freight between the two coasts, primarily serving American interests. But in 1881, the French bought the controlling interest because the railroad was to play a major role in their building of a sea level canal. As you already know from an earlier chapter, the French company went bankrupt, leaving the railroad unmanaged and in a position to deteriorate under the tropical sun and given the high humidity. But in 1904, the United States bought the French assets and began to restore the railroad. Today the railroad handles local freight between the two major cities, but it also carries canal workers and local residents across the isthmus, operating very nice quality passenger coaches. In 2001, a major restoration and upgrade took place, a project that took several years to complete. Freight is still an important source of revenue for the railroad, but passenger traffic is also significant.

Many tourists who are visiting Panama City will often ride the train over to Colón and back just to have a better look at the canal.

As the city has deteriorated because of a loss of economic significance and politically being ignored, most of its once wealthy families have relocated to Panama City. The primary population today is a mix of West Indian and Panamanians of the peasant classes, primarily menial workers and their families.

WHAT TO SEE: You may at this point wonder why a cruise ship would stop here, and that would be a fair question. The purpose is to enable passengers to choose from among several tour options that give you a chance to see some of Panama as a country. When transiting through the canal, you catch glimpses of Panama City's skyline and you see the tropical rainforest along the shores of the Chagres River and Gatun Lake. But there is much more to Panama that is otherwise missed. Here are some of the possibilities that are offered by cruise lines during a port call in Colón:

* Spend much of the day touring Panama City. The national capital and most vibrant city in Central America is only an hour by motor coach from Colón. On an all day tour you have a chance to see some of the rainforest country while en route, and then visit the old, historic districts and the modern beachfront portions of Panama City

* Wildlife - There are various reserves close to the canal, or on some of the islands created by Gatun Lake. Many shore excursions will include visits to several of the island reserves to see monkeys and bird life.

* Gamboa Aerial Tram - A chance to take an aerial ride through a portion of rainforest, but at treetop level has great appeal to those with some spirit of adventure.

* Gatun Lake cruises enable you to enjoy both the scenery and the wildlife, as this type of tour overlaps the wildlife tours through stops to observe monkeys and birds.

* A tour of the Panamanian countryside gives those who do not wish to engage in much walking or spend time on small boats a chance to see the beautiful landscapes of Panama, but more in passing.

* A look at Panama Canal operations - This is a tour where you get to see the workings of the Panama Canal from the landward side, which is a totally different perspective than you have from on board the ship.

If your cruise includes an all day stop in Colón, I highly recommend that you book one of the ship's excursions otherwise you will find it to be a long day with nothing to do. Visiting Colón on your own is not recommended, as this is a depressed city where you could easily become a victim of a criminal act. Thus taking one of the tours is the only way to maximize the day unless your choice is to soak up the tropical sun by the ship's pool.

The passenger train between Panama City and Colón

Cruising the back waters of Gatun Lake

VISITING COSTA RICA

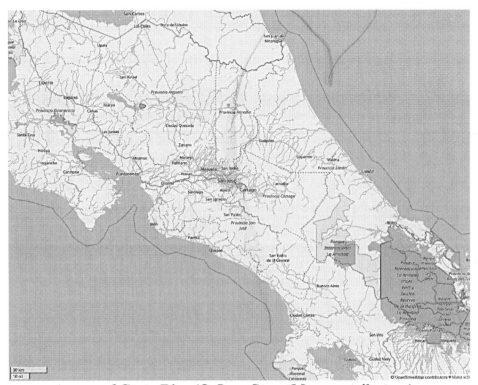

A map of Costa Rica (© OpenStreetMap contributors)

I must admit that my personal choice of the Central American countries is Costa Rica. This small nation has the highest overall standard of living in the region when viewed relative to the distribution of wealth, and it has the highest literacy rate in Latin America. Essentially Costa Rica is a middle class, very democratic and peaceful nation, the only one in the region that does not maintain a military. Crime rates are low and life is essentially calm and people appear to be very content with their lives. The Republic of Costa Rica is located north of Panama and south of Nicaragua, occupying a relatively narrow strip of land between the Caribbean Sea to the east and the Pacific Ocean to the west. The country extends over 50,901 square kilometers or 19,653 square miles, making about the size of the American state of South Carolina or the European nation of Estonia. The population of Costa Rica is 5,057,000 at last count. Most of the nation's inhabitants are of pure European stock, mainly from Spain, accounting for 74 percent of the total population. This is one of the four highest pure European populations in Latin America, the other nations being Argentina, Chile and Uruguay. And it is important to note that all four have the highest overall standards of living within Latin America. In the remainder of the countries, the majority of the predominantly mixed race population is dominated over by a small, elite class of people with stronger Iberian bloodlines.

What also greatly distinguishes Costa Rica is the national policy regarding care of the environment. When it comes to developing a policy of environmental sustainability, Costa Rica is the highest ranking in the Americas as the fifth highest-ranking nation in the world. The government pledged to become totally carbon neutral by 2021, and is well on its way to achieving that goal. The country is also a leader in the whole concept of ecotourism. Some actually claim that Costa Rica created the very concept.

Most cruise ship visits to Costa Rica that are part of a Panama Canal transit are based upon one port call on the Pacific Coast, generally the port of Puntarenas. A very few cruise lines stop in Puerto Limón on the Caribbean coast as part of a canal transit, but many cruise lines include this port as part of their western Caribbean cruise itineraries. I will briefly comment on Puerto Limón in this chapter in the event a reader happens to be on a cruise that will visit that port, but most of my attention will focus upon Puntarenas and the various all day shore excursions from that Pacific port.

THE NATURAL LANDSCAPE: Given the importance of Costa Rica as the most important country in the Western Hemisphere for its environmental policies and ecotourism, it is important to look at the natural environment.

The majority of the nation's people live in a central plateau, which is actually a series of interconnecting valleys separated from both coasts by parallel ranges of mountains. This pattern extends from Mexico right through the heart of Central America. The Cordillera Central and Talamanca form the main mountain spine of the nation along with shorter intervening ranges. The highest peak is just over 3,810 meters or 12,500 feet above sea level. The majority of the high mountain peaks of Costa Rica are volcanic, and many are quite active. There is always the danger of a volcanic eruption with intensities that can be relatively devastating. In the north of the country is Volcan Arenal, which is the most active in the country and has had dozens of significant eruptions in the past 45 years. Along with volcanic eruptions, the country is also subjected to frequent earthquakes many of which can also be relatively devastating. Both the volcanic and seismic activity result from the entire region being located adjacent to a major plate boundary where one plate is subducting, or sliding under the other. As the sea plate subducts, it melts and creates vast reservoirs of magma that then can trigger volcanic eruptions when the pressures reach a critical level.

Although the people of Costa Rica live with active volcanoes and are subjected to earthquakes, the land has been greatly enriched in vital nutrients by the flows of lava and ash fallout over millennia. And they have learned to live with these dangers, accepting them as a fact of life.

The tropical latitude of Costa Rica makes this a tropical nation, but the high elevations moderate the climate, making the interior valleys of the plateau quite pleasant and comfortable. Rainfall is very reliable and combined with the good soils and moderate temperatures; produce a virtual "Garden of Eden." But as one proceeds to the coast, the temperature and humidity intensify, making the coastal environment far less livable. Fortunately the Pacific coastal margin has both a wet and dry season, and the shorelines are punctuated by sea breezes that make the weather tolerable. On the Caribbean coast, the land is flat extending inland 50 to 100 miles until it reaches the main cordillera. Onshore Trade Winds bring copious quantities of precipitation, often enhanced by tropical hurricanes. This is a difficult region to inhabit because the thick rainforest is not easily penetrated, and the hot and humid climate is not seen as overly desirable. And along with the heat and high humidity come mosquitos and other noxious insect pests.

Because of its many life zones resulting from elevation changes, Costa Rica is a country with a great biodiversity. There are over 12,000 native species of plants ranging from tall forest trees that produce a thick canopy to hundreds of delicate flowers. On the western side of the Cordillera is the Monteverde Cloud Forest, one of the most distinctive ecological zones in the country. Here most inflowing air is forced to rise and condense, creating an almost daily layer of fog or high cloud that nourishes a rich ecosystem.

Over the years much of the mountain and high valley forest has been removed to clear land for ranching and farming. But since the mid 20th century, Costa Ricans have become great stewards of the land. Today over 25 percent of the total land area is protected as environmental reserve land.

The animal life of Costa Rica also exhibits great diversity. Hundreds of species of reptiles, amphibians, birds and mammals along with over 180 species of fish add to the biodiversity of this small nation. And the government has put a total ban on hunting to enable the nation's wildlife to thrive without intervention. Introduced cattle appear to be the most commonplace animal you will see in the countryside, as much of the highland valley country was cleared of its original forest cover.

HISTORY: Costa Rica has seen a totally different historic development than its other Central American neighbors. Initially during prehistoric times, this was a peripheral region inhabited by simplistic hunting and gathering peoples widely scattered over the land. The few tribal groups that existed when the Spanish arrived were either decimated by diseases or slowly infused into the cultural matrix through intermarriage to where today only 13.6 percent of the population would be classified as mestizo, meaning that they have part native blood. Unlike other Central American countries where the natives and mestizo populations remained poor and were exploited by the pure Hispanic class, a condition still prevalent today, this was never the case for Costa Rica.

Even during the Spanish colonial period, Costa Rica was considered to be a distant frontier province, as the regional authorities were located to the north in Guatemala. Under the laws governing the vast Viceroyalty of New Spain, Costa Rica was not able to engage in trade with lands to the south that were part of the Viceroyalty of New Granada. Thus it faced a degree of isolation, and furthermore, it had little to offer. Gold, silver or other precious metals were lacking, and its rich farm and ranch land was not valued at the time. It also lacked a native population that could be exploited since there were no mines and farming and ranching was more of a subsistence activity. In the end the province was looked upon as an impoverished backwater.

Left alone, the Costa Rican settlers placed great value upon education and cooperation, essentially becoming a people who favored local home rule, setting the stage for a different brand of independence when it finally came on the heels of Mexican independence declared in 1821. Initially Costa Rica joined the ill-fated Mexican Empire, but by 1823 that entity had essentially imploded. The next experiment was the equally unsuccessful Federal Republic of Central America, which lasted from 1823 to 1839. Costa Rica was still considered to be the most impoverished of the component states. Costa Rica withdrew from the Central American confederation in 1838, preferring to become totally independent even though this meant a greater degree of isolation from their neighbors. But throughout the Spanish colonial era and while a member of the federation, Costa Rica was always on the fringe, and it was essentially isolated.

The country's main cash crop to bring in hard currency was coffee, exported via the Pacific. Colorful oxcarts brought the beans down from the highlands to Puntarenas. Then the coffee beans faced the long route around the tip of South America and onward to Europe. What the country needed was a railroad to the Caribbean coast. From start to completion, it took 20-years for the project to be concluded in 1890. The mountainous route down to the coastal plain combined with the tropical heat and disease of the lowlands made this a difficult project. The project employed Jamaican along with a mix of Chinese and Italian immigrants, and the builder, a United States businessman won large tracts of land. He in turn started banana plantations, often employing the former railway workers, and the coastal town of Limón became a rather unsavory place of residence and commercial activity. This image plagues the town today despite it being Costa Rica's window to the Caribbean.

By the start of the 20th century, Costa Rica was considered to be one of the banana republics, heavily influenced by United Fruit Company's dominance over the purchasing and shipping of the crop out of Limón.

When viewed relative to other Latin American nations, Costa Rica's history as an independent nation has been quite peaceful. There was a brief overthrow of General Granados in 1919, after his two-year dictatorial rule. Then a disputed presidential election in 1948 led to a 44-day civil war that resulted in over 2,000 deaths -

the worst event in the country's history. The new government dismissed the military and to the present Costa Rica has only a civil police force and no armed forces. The new constitution approved in 1953, has given the nation total stability. There has been no violence since and elections are held openly and peacefully. The nation also looks after its people by providing good schools, medical clinics and attempts to make certain that there is a minimal welfare net to provide for its people.

Costa Rica has preserved much of its rainforest

Bananas are still important to the Caribbean coast of Costa Rica

The dry season in the Pacific mountains of Costa Rica

The highland valleys are green year around

LIMÓN

This Caribbean port is on few itineraries that include a transit of the Panama Canal. Many western Caribbean cruises, however, stop here as part of an attempt to include Costa Rica in the itinerary. But frankly there is little or nothing of interest in Puerto Limón to discuss. Tours out of the town will include visits to nature reserves protecting the Caribbean forest environment, or visits to a banana plantation. And the most energetic of all tours is one that makes the rather lengthy mountain ascent to visit San José, which frankly is too tedious for a single day's adventure. If your cruise ship is also going to stop in Puntarenas on the Pacific side of Costa Rica, a journey to San José from that port takes only 90 minutes.

You may be surprised to learn that with only 56,000 residents, Limón is the second largest city in Costa Rica after the national capital of San José. Limón has a somewhat ramshackle appearance, typical of most of the towns on the Caribbean side of Central America. These towns have served as ports and trade centers for the banana plantations, and some have actually developed an unsavory reputation. The reputation for vice, prostitution and drugs has also to some degree applied to Limón in that it is not typical of Costa Rica when contrasted to the upland valleys where the majority of the population lives.

The coastline is relatively flat with numerous swamps and mangroves, a landscape that is made up of scrub woodlands, some rainforest and many fresh water streams coming down from the mountains. The weather is hot and humid most of the year, and the region is prone to being struck by hurricanes every few years. It has never been seen by Costa Ricans as a desirable place to live, especially centuries back when tropical diseases were the scourge of all who lived in these locales.

HISTORIC SKETCH: Limón has a rather mixed population resulting from the history of its growth. There is a mix of Jamaicans, Chinese and other Caribbean people, giving this area a cultural mix quite different from the nation as a whole. These people came in during the late 19th century as workers on the railroad that was built to connect Limón with the capital up in the highlands. In these early decades, the Costa Rican government had a travel ban on people of non-European ethnicity, barring them from moving into the core area of the country.

During the early Spanish history in Central America the coastal plains along the Caribbean were seen as very undesirable. But even with the government willing to grant tracts of lands, most Spaniards chose not to settle. The few who did settle imported African slaves and planted cocoa as their cash crop.

Limón was founded in 1854 to be the starting point for the railroad into the interior so that Costa Rica's valuable coffee could be exported abroad. The city also became the Costa Rican base of operations for United Fruit Company, holder of vast banana plantations.

The city's distinct ethnic makeup, which tends to have a more Caribbean vibe is the result of the descendants of former slaves mixing with the workers who came from the Caribbean islands to work on the railroad. And the white population is also more a mix of Italian, British and American than it is of Spanish or Mestiso. More common than Spanish as the language of Limón, it is actually a Creole base with heavy use of English.

WHAT TO SEE OR DO: If you stay in Limón, you will find that after an hour of walking the somewhat typically Caribbean main street, you will be bored and end up back on the ship. To make the most of a day in Limón, take one of your ship's tours, as they have a strong ecological base and this is what Costa Rican tourism is truly about. The coastal plain does have some very interesting vegetation and animal life, so get out and enjoy the landscape. The main sites that are usually visited include:
* Tortugero National Park - A mix of coastal and rainforest landscapes blended together by nature, and a beautiful place for a nature walk. The park is open daily from 8 AN to Noon and from 1 to 4 PM.
* Cahuita National Park - South of Limón, this is another national park along the coast where plant and animal species of two biospheres inter mix. The park is open daily from 8 AM to 4 PM.
* Veragua Rainforest Park - Close to the city, this park gives you a good look at the tropical rainforest through interpretative guides, as you walk through its trees. The park is open Tuesday thru Sunday from 8 AM to 3 PM.

* Foundation Jaguar Rescue Center - This is a major animal rescue and rehabilitation center for the Jaguar, the region's small carnivore, similar in nature to a cheetah. The center is in South Puerto Viejo, which is south of Limón. It is open from 9 AM to 2:30 PM daily except Sunday/

DINING OUT: If you are on an all day tour, lunch is usually included. If you take a half-day tour, you can either go back into Limón for lunch or remain on board ship. I would say that Limón is not a gourmet center, and do not have any one restaurant I would recommend. There are several nice restaurants along the coast north and south of Limón, and these often are venues for lunch on all day tours. But within Limón I believe you are better off dining on board ship.

SHOPPING: Costa Rica is noted for its fine woodcarvings, painted wood miniature ox carts, woven wares and leather. But the best shopping is found in the central highlands. However, in Limón, there is the Mercado Municipal in the center of town. It is a typical Caribbean and quasi Latin American marketplace. You will find some craft items here. The majority of nice shops selling local crafts are located in or adjacent to the national parks, and if you go on tour, often the bus will stop at one of these venues and give you some time to shop.

FINAL WORDS: Take advantage of any opportunity in Costa Rica to maximize your time and see as much of the country, or its coastal rainforests because this is the nation that prides itself in eco tourism and is so highly recognized worldwide as a leader in the realm of carbon neutral living As for the city of Limón, just accept it as what it is and do not think of it as being typically Costa Rican.

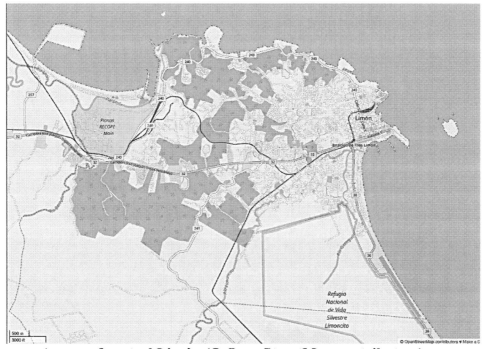

A map of central Limón (© OpenStreetMap contributors)

The ramshackle nature of Limón (Work of Balou46, CC BT SA 4.0, Wikimedia.org)

The main street of Limón (Work of Balou46, CC BT SA 4.0, Wikimedia.org)

Limón is a very laid back town (Work of Balou46, CC BY SA 4.0, Wikimedia.org

PUNTARENAS

The majority of cruise ships stop at Puntarenas on the Gulf of Nicoya along the Pacific Coast. There is a single pier located in Puntarenas that leads from the ship to the center of the city. But this pier cannot accommodate the large cruise ships that most passengers who transit the Panama Canal happen to be on. Only smaller ships for such cruise lines as Silversea, Seaborne or Regent Seven Seas will dock at the main central pier. The larger ships dock a few miles south in a new port facility that serves for heavy freight traffic for the populated centers in the interior. If Puerto Caldera is listed in your itinerary, your ship will dock in what is essentially a container port. And with some cruise lines, they list the port as Puntarenas, but it is actually Puerto Caldera.

Puntarenas is a city of just over 34,000 people, but it serves a surrounding area of approximately 110,000 residents. The city only dates to 1840 when coffee exports from the central highlands necessitated a port and this site was chosen. It is on the Gulf of Nicoya, thus sheltered from the open Pacific and made for a good anchorage. By the late 20th century, the port facilities in Puntarenas had begun to deteriorate, and the new port facility at Caldera was built and today handles the bulk of the Pacific traffic. The city of Puntarenas has little to nothing to offer a cruise ship passenger if they elect not to participate in one of the all day tours available. In my personal opinion, the ramshackle architecture and lack of nice shops or restaurants in many ways discredits all that has thus far been said about the progressive nature and middle class values of Costa Rica. Thus I highly urge all readers to strongly consider one of the tours to see and appreciate the land and people of Costa Rica.

These are the standard tours available when your ship is docked in Puntarenas or Puerto Caldera:
* Monteverde Cloud Forest - One of the most spectacular of national parks in Costa Rica, this high altitude tropical rainforest is located at such an elevation that when moist air is intercepted by the surrounding peaks, the forest is shrouded in clouds. A full section discussing the beauty of the cloud forest will be found later in the chapter. It is my number one recommendation with regard to a tour when in Puntarenas. If you visit Monteverde, you will gain a true appreciation for the beauty of the tropical rainforest.

* Poas Volcano - The largest volcanic caldera in Costa Rica, Poas is today simply simmering and has not staged any massive eruptions in recent decades. The potential for a major eruption is ever present, as Poas steams and puffs and ejects occasional dark clouds, but more often simply massive jets of steam and boiling water. This is such a major site and so popular that it will also be discussed farther along in the chapter. The park is open daily from 7 AM to 4 PM.

* Eco Tours - Depending upon the arrangements made by your cruise line, there are numerous eco tour options from Puntarenas. It is possible to do a zip lining adventure at Los Sueños, the famous Pacific Rim Aerial Tram through the rainforest canopy, a mangrove or rainforest river journey down the Guacalillo Estuary, the Tarcoles River or the Corobici River.

* A jungle crocodile boat ride on the Tarcoles River may sound touristy, but it is a valid nature oriented tour. You will see wild crocodiles and actually get up close to them.

* A leisurely few hours relaxing at the Miravalles Hot Springs resort in the central highlands is a nice way to spend the day if you have already been to Costa Rica and would like to just spend a relaxed day ashore.

* A visit to Sarchi - This small central highland town is filled with artisan studios where they produce the beautiful hand-painted oxcarts that once served to transport the coffee beans from the highlands. Today the studios produce miniature oxcarts, umbrellas and other hand-painted craft items for visitors. This is a popular short trip for those truly interested in traditional crafts, and it gives you a chance to visit a typical central valley community

A visit to San José - The capital and largest city of Costa Rica is San José, located in the central plateau region of the country, surrounded on the east and west by mountains, many of which are active volcanoes. This city of 2,158,000 residents is the true heart of the nation. Because of the many things to see and do in the capital, it will be treated as a separate entry later in this chapter. Normally cruise lines offer a full day tour to San José, which by expressway is just over one hour from Puntarenas.

MONTEVERDE CLOUD FOREST: Located about two hours northeast of Puntarenas, much of the journey via unpaved, but smooth road, this is the gem of the national parks of the nation. The drive to and from the national park is very dramatic, as the changes in altitude reveal the different layers of vegetation that make up the landscape. Monteverde is at over 1,524 meters or 5,000 feet above sea level in the Cordillera de Tilarán where it intercepts warm inflowing Pacific air laden with moisture. As the air cools and condenses, clouds form, but right over the mountaintop, draping this thick rainforest in evening and morning fog and drizzle. It is haunting and very ethereal. Some even say it is "spooky," but that is a rather juvenile term, yet effective in describing the landscape.

The park is home to 2,500 species of plants including the largest number of orchids found in any one location, 400 species of birds, 120 reptilian species and 100 species of mammals. There are also numerous insect species, but none that are pesky to visitors.

A special narrow gauge train takes visitors on nature rides through the park. But there are also hiking trails and zip lining facilities. A small hotel, gift shop and restaurant offer comforts for the visitor. Most cruise tours generally include a traditional Costa Rican lunch of roasted meats, chicken, rice, beans, bananas and salad, topped off by freshly brewed highland coffee and dessert. And remember that in Costa Rica sanitation is at a much higher level than elsewhere in Latin America. You can eat with confidence that you will not experience any intestinal upset, but to play safe, do not eat anything raw.

POAS VOLCANO: There are many active volcanoes in Costa Rica, Arenal being the most famous and explosive of the peaks. But Poas Volcano is a massive caldera, an expansive crater containing several vents, representing past explosive eruptions of unimagined fury. Today the volcano is relatively calm; most of its activity is in the form of steam eruptions, with occasional outbursts of lava over the lip of one of its smaller interior craters. But there is still the potential for a violent eruption to occur even though it is probably very unlikely. Volcanoes must always be treated with respect for their fury is uncontrollable. Many times at the rim of the Poas Crater, it will be foggy just as in the Monteverde Cloud Forest. You will smell the sulphur gasses and hear the steam vents, but you may not be able to see in front of your hand.

Poas Volcano is just north of greater San José, the route taking you just through the northern suburbs of the capital. The massive bulk of Poas Volcano rises to a height of 2,708 meters or 8,885 feet. Its northern crater lake is filled with highly acidic water at high temperatures, often producing clouds of acid fog and rain. The southern lake is fresh because that crater is inactive.

Normally the drive to Poas takes about two hours, and you see the changes in the landscape from the coastal wet and dry forest to the central highland woodlands and the coffee plantations, many of them on terraced lower slopes of the volcano. Then after spending a couple of hours at the summit, lunch is provided at one of several local country restaurants. Some cruise tours will return by way of the arts and crafts city of Sarchi.

SAN JOSÉ: After a scenic one-hour or slightly longer drive along the country's new expressway, climbing rapidly through the western coastal mountains, you will arrive in the vibrant and bustling capital of Costa Rica. Metropolitan San José is the capital, cultural center and also the most important commercial city in the nation. The foothill suburb of Escazu is a community that has attracted numerous expatriate Americans who have chosen to retire to Costa Rica. It is the most modern and beautiful of the various communities that make up the capital. San Miguel de Escazu occupies the southern foothill slopes of greater San José and can be recognized as you enter the city by noting its modern high-rise condominium and apartment blocks that rise out of the surrounding canopy of trees that shade the suburban streets.

San José is quite unlike any of the other capitals in Central America. It is the most prosperous, yet not in any extravagant way, as it represents the greater equity between wealth and poverty than what is seen in neighboring countries. There are fewer grand palatial mansions in San José and likewise a very small area that would be classed as a poverty stricken barrio. The major residential quarters of the city are composed of small, neat homes representing the vast middle class majority. Around the city center, these houses are clustered together in rows, as the buildings date to the colonial era. They are often brightly painted or done in muted pastels, showing an outer wall and barred windows, typical of colonial decor. In the outer suburbs, the houses are individual, generally built of concrete and are surrounded by limited yards and foliage.

Keep in mind that San José is situated in a high frequency earthquake zone as well as being in the shadow of two major volcanoes whose period eruptions shower the city with ash and pumice. There are signs in almost every public venue that points out what to do during an earthquake. The people are very accepting of this natural hazard and also of the periodic ash showers.

Downtown San José is exceptionally clean. But since this was considered a frontier outpost during colonial times, there are few grand buildings that date back to the early Spanish era. There are, however, several beautiful examples of Costa Rican public architecture from the 19th century.

Here are the major sights your tour, be it a group coach excursion or a private car and driver/guide, should include:
* The Metropolitan Cathedral - This baroque cathedral is not as grand as others in Latin America, but it is still a traditional house of worship and faces one of the city's main plazas.
* Teatro Nacional de Costa Rica - This elegant, but small opera house is the pride of the city, dating to 1897 during the height of the coffee plantation era. Located at Avenida Dos and Calle Cinco. If not attending a performance, the building is generally open for visitors to walk through during daylight hours.
* Correo de Costa Rica - The 19th century post and telegraph building is one of the finest examples of grand public architecture in Central America . The building is open for business during normal hours of 8 AM to 6 PM on weekdays.
* Mercado Central - This is the grand food market located in the city center. It is exceptionally clean, yet filled with a lot of local color and charm, and it shows you what is available to eat in the country. Located between Avenida Central and Avenida 1 and between Calle Seis and Calle Ocho. It is open daily from 6:30 AM to 5:45 PM except Sunday.
* Museo Nacional de Costa Rica - This is the country's great museum of natural history and culture, showcasing the nation. Located on Calle 17 between Avenida Central and Segunda. The museum is open Tuesday thru Saturday from 8:30 AM to 4:30 PM and opens Sunday at 9 AM until 4:30 PM.
* Museo de Arte Costarirricense - This is a beautiful museum of national arts and crafts. It is located in the Parque Metropolitano.

*The Museum of Pre Colombian Gold - A good collection of gold objects from the Maya and other civilizations of the Americas, though none existed in Costa Rica. Located on Calle Cinco between Avenida Central and Avenida Segundo. The museum is open from 0 AM to 4 PM Tuesday thru Sunday.

* La Plaza de Cultura - Opposite the opera house, this is the most popular and active plaza in the central city.

* The Simón Bolivar Zoo - Noted for its variety of Costa Rican wildlife and birds. The zoo is open from 9 AM to 4:30 PM daily.

SHOPPING: Puntarenas is not a place where you will find much shopping. There is one store in the town center called LimeCoral Jaco Shop on Calle Jaco Sol that does sell local craft items and souvenirs.

In The Monteverde Cloud Forest you will have a brief opportunity to shop for local crafts in the hotel where you have lunch. And depending upon time, your tour coach may stop at one roadside souvenir store.

On the Poas Volcano tour, most coaches will return via the small town of Sarchi. Here you will find the best-known arts and crafts guild in Costa Rica. They are famous for their hand painted miniature ox carts that are truly representative of the country.

In San José there are good quality arts and crafts for sale in the Mercado Publico, which is a major city center attraction. There are numerous small galleries that sell local arts and crafts located in the city center:

* Galeria Namu on Avenida Siete between Calle Cinco and Siete is an excellent shop for indigenous arts. They are open from 8 AM to 6:30 PM daily, and on Sunday from 1 to 5 PM, January thru April.

* Holalola Souvenir Shop on Los Yoses Boulevard is known for its fine quality handmade Costa Rican souvenirs. Unfortunately they do not appear to post their hours on their web page.

DINING OUT: On any of the all day tours, lunch will be served at a predetermined restaurant where you simply have no choice. But the cruise lines are careful to choose restaurants that are both of a high standard and offer traditional Costa Rican cuisine. Normally meat such as beef, chicken or pork will be served with beans and rice, plantains fried in butter and one or more vegetables. Dessert is

116

almost always tres leches cake, a rich confection with three kinds of milk including heavy cream and whipped cream.

In San José if you do happen to go on your own, I recommend the following restaurants for lunch:

* Restaurant la Terrasse - This excellent fine dining establishment is in an old house on Avenida Nueve just south of the Hotel la Amistad. This will be a gourmet Costa Rican lunch. Open Monday thru Friday from Noon to 2 PM and 7 to 10 PM for dinner. Saturday they are open from 7 to 10 for dinner. Closed Sunday.

* Taller Gastronómico el Punto - At 75 M Oeste del Blue Valley on the northwestern edge of Escazu, this is one of the most artful and innovative dining establishments where lunch is a work of art. Most guests are shocked at the novel and elegant cuisine that is served. They are open Tuesday thru Friday from Noon to 10 PM, Monday only for dinner from 7 to 10 PM and Saturday from 1 to 10 PM.

* La Esquina de Buenos Aires - Downtown at Calle Once at the corner of Avenida has a very good menu. Open Tuesday thru Thursday from 11:30 AM to 3 PM and 6 to 10:30 PM, Friday from 11:30 AM to 11 PM. Saturday 12:30 to 11 PM, Sunday Noon to 10 PM.

Quatro, this is a restaurant for meat eaters. It features the flavor and style of its namesake Buenos Aires, but this same style of preparation for meat is also typical to Costa Rica. Open daily from 6:30 AM to Midnight.

FINAL NOTE: A visit to Puntarenas gives you several opportunities to visit different parts of Costa Rica, varying from the national capital city to a massive volcanic crater to a mountain cloud forest. It is one of the most diverse stops you will find on the entire cruise. Puntarenas just happens to be central to so many distinct venues, each with its own specific climatic zone. The only problem with such a one-day visit is trying to choose where to go. I recommended several venues because over the years I have sampled them all. It depends upon your specific taste. In the end, you can always take a local taxi to one of the beautiful beaches outside of Puntarenas and simply have a relaxing day.

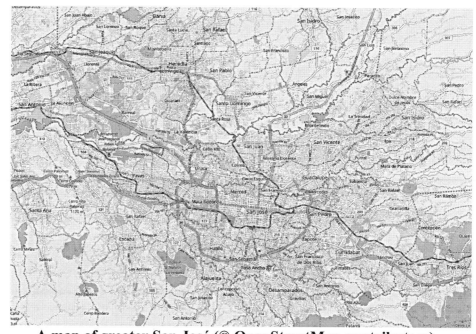

A map of greater San José (© OpenStreetMap contributors)

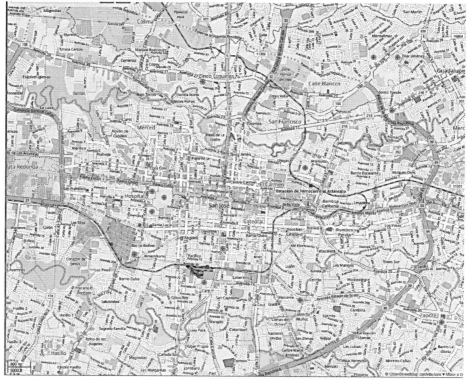

A map of central San José (© OpenStreetMap contributors)

118

Docking on the long pier in Puntarenas

En route to the Monteverde Cloud Forest

In the Monteverde Cloud Forest

The miniature Monteverde Cloud Forest railway

The Autopista to the interior of Costa Rica from Puntarenas

Countryside en route from Puntarenas to San José

Steaming cauldron of Poas Volcano (Work of Peloy (Allan H. M.), CC BY SA 3.0, Wikimedia.org)

The richly forested slopes above San José

Plaza de la Cultura in downtown San José

Avenida Central in San José

Teatro Nacional in downtown San José

Colonial architecture of the Post Office in downtown San Jos

One of the colorful oxcarts made in the town of Sarchi

In the small highland town of Grecia

VISITING GUATEMALA

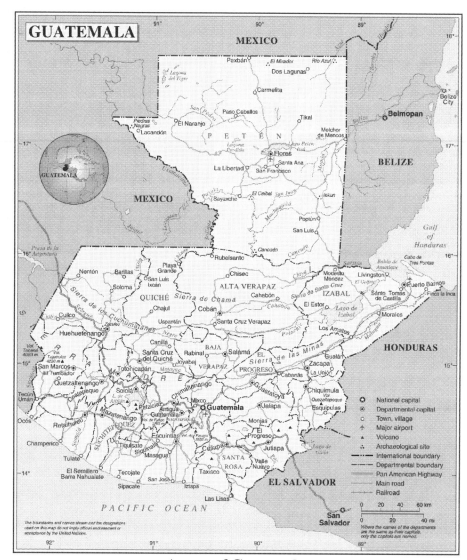

A map of Guatemala

Guatemala has made the newspapers and television in the past year with regard to the high rate of violence perpetrated against the peasant population by both the military and drug cartels, giving the impression that it is not safe for visitors. This impression would hold true for any tourist wanting to go and explore the backwater areas of the country. But when you are part of an organized group excursion offered by your cruise line, you are in no danger whatever. I have been to Guatemala numerous times by ship, and although I prefer going out on my own, I refrained and instead took ship tours and still came away with a good understanding of the country on each visit. And when you are in a major destination such as Antigua or Tikal, you can feel free to explore on your own for an hour or two with no danger, as the tours are organized in such a way as to give you some independent time.

Guatemala is a much larger country than Costa Rica, having 108,888 square kilometers or 42,042 square miles and a population of over 15,800,000. In physical size the country is as large as the American state of Pennsylvania or slightly larger than the European nations of Austria or Hungary. It is located along the southern border of Mexico, adjacent to Belize and Honduras, having its primary sea access along the Pacific coast, but also with a small window on the Caribbean Sea.

Cruise ships stop in Puerto Quetzal, a commercial port located on the Pacific coastal plain, giving easy access to the historic colonial city of Antigua or the capital of Guatemala City. There is a local airport that provides charter flights to the far north of the country for one day visits to the ancient Maya ruins of Tikal. Other one-day trips are made from Puerto Quetzal to one of the active volcanoes or to Copan across the border in western Honduras. And some cruise lines offer a very exhausting one-day coach trip to Lake Atitlan.

PHYSICAL ENVIRONMENT: Like Costa Rica, the physical landscape of the core of Guatemala is the same. There is a coastal plain on the Pacific side, followed by a cordillera that leads to an upland plateau that is essentially a series of interconnecting valleys. There is a second cordillera that separates the north of the country, which is part of the vast, limestone Yucatan plain. The orientation of the entire country is on an east to west axis, with the Pacific coast to the south and the Yucatan and the Caribbean Sea to the north.

Guatemala is a volatile land when it comes to earthquake and volcanic activity. The core of the country lies along a fault zone that separates the North American and Caribbean Plates. A third plate, called Cocos, lies off the south coast in the Pacific Ocean. It is subducting below the Caribbean Plate, creating numerous active volcanoes. The highest peak in all of Central America, the volcano Tajumulco is over 4,220 meters or 13,845 feet high. There are also several deep interior lakes, each filling a volcanic caldera, set amid the volcanic field, the most famous being Lake Atitlan. The scenic beauty of the lake and its surrounding volcanoes belies the potential for a catastrophic event in the near future. Past catastrophic earthquakes have destroyed the cities of Antigua and Guatemala City, and the danger looms on the horizon for the future.

Northern Guatemala is flat, covered in a stunted forest or woodland and lacks flowing rivers because of its underlying limestone structure that acts as a giant sponge to soak in the rainwater. Yet it was here that the once mighty Maya civilization once flourished. Northern Guatemala is also within the path of potential hurricanes and has seen its share of such disasters.

A BRIEF HISTORY: The history of Guatemala is critical to appreciating the various potential sights to be seen during your one-day visit. This is a nation steeped in Pre-Colombian history followed by a long Spanish colonial heritage. The country was once home to major civilization and then became the political and cultural heart of Central America during Spanish rule. Thus whatever you choose to do in Guatemala by way of taking a field trip, you will be exposed to some aspect of its history.

People have been living in what is now Guatemala for over 14,000 years. Cultivation is believed to have begun around 5,500 years ago, but it was the Maya civilization that reached its great heights of architectural and scientific development around the start of the historic calendar. Maya influences spread throughout the highlands, and after the collapse of their great cities in the Yucatan, smaller highland civilizations continued Mayan traditions.

The Spanish began to explore south from central Mexico and by the early 1520's, Guatemala became an important province of New Spain, but it was plagued by natural disasters. Between 1520 and 1541, the capital had to move twice as the prior settlements were devastated by native attacks, earthquake or flood. Finally Antigua became the capital. But it too was heavily devastated in 1773 and 1774 by earthquakes, finally forcing a third move to what is today Guatemala City. But Antigua had been capital long enough to have developed magnificent colonial architecture, and despite rebuilding, it still managed to retain its importance. Today it is a UNESCO World Heritage Site.

It was Guatemala that in 1821 led the independence movement, then uniting the former provinces into the Central American Federation. But it dissolved by 1840, but not until civil war had first erupted in most of the member provinces. Internally Guatemala went through decades of dictatorships and revolutions. In 1871, under the leadership of Justo Rufino Barrios, the country started to modernize, develop a road infrastructure and manufacturing. Like Costa Rica, first coffee and then bananas became important commercial crops. And United Fruit Company was very instrumental in maintaining Manuel Estrada Cabrera as dictator for 22 years until 1920. From July through October 1944, the country was in turmoil after the ouster of one dictator, replaced by a general and then a military junta. Finally the first freely elected president, Juan Bermejo, managed to keep in office for his full term, reforming the role of workers. Jacobo Guzmán then succeeded him in 1951, and he brought about many land reforms. However the next government was overthrown by a coup d'état promulgated by the CIA, fearing that the new President Árbenz was a socialist, this at a time when the United States was frantic in its fears over Communism. In 1954, General Armas, with CIA aid, invaded from Honduras, but it did not take long for him to be assassinated in 1957. The next president still had American support, and he was instrumental in providing an airstrip for the ill-fated Bay of Pigs invasion in 1961 and the training of 5,000 anti-Castro forces on Guatemalan soil. But of course this government did not last long, the next coup being led by the Defense Minister in 1963 after the failed Bay of Pigs fiasco. This coup also had American backing, and it led to a terror campaign against former President Ydígoras-Fuentes who had been previously ousted.

It was not until 1966 that free elections were held. The new president was left leaning and rightist groups formed paramilitary units that received open assistance and training from the United States Army. Again chaos reigned, as the 1970 presidential election was contested and several guerrilla groups began to take a foothold in several rural areas. Again in 1974, the election was disputed and this led to tension and instability. Nature intervened in 1975 with a massive earthquake that killed over 25,000 people, many having died in substandard housing that simply collapsed. The government did little to aid the people, and this ultimately caused great unrest, which was further enhanced by a fraudulent election in 1978.

Guatemala entered a terrible period in which guerrilla groups terrorized the nation, which brought swift responses from the military. In 1979, the United States suspended all military aid, however, clandestine aid still filtered in to the government. The people were essentially caught in the middle. In 1982, after a brutal attack on the Spanish Embassy by guerrilla groups was met with a governmental assault, the government was overthrown and a new military junta was formed. However, the conditions remained the same with torture, murder and burning of villages to root out the guerrilla groups. Conditions were so bad, especially after the four guerrilla groups merged into one powerful command, that thousands of peasants took refuge in southern Mexico, assisted by that government.

It was not until 1986 that another coup brought about a new constitution and free elections. But it was not until 1996 that the so-called civil war ended with the United Nations brokering a peace between the guerrilla group and the government. Both the military and the paramilitary groups were blamed for their share in the violence and abuses during this brutal period. The brutality began as an offensive against the intellectual class, but in the end it turned ethnic with a heavy degree of persecution against the Maya who make up a great percentage of the rural population. As many as a quarter million are believed to have died, a further million displaced and many dozens of villages burned, with the military having been the greatest perpetrator. Many blame the United States for having supported the succession of military governments from the early 1950's until the early 1980's. In the name of keeping Communism at bay, the Americans helped fan the flames of brutality in Guatemala, something that the Clinton administration did finally acknowledge.

This very brief history shows you how tragic life in Guatemala has been for the vast majority since the 1940's. Only now is the country starting to develop some semblance of an infrastructure and democratic elections. But now drug violence has started to take its toll of the rural population in particular, as Guatemala has a favored environment for raising marijuana and coca. Some manufacturing has been fostered, especially in Guatemala City, and several mineral processing plants have been built in Puerto Quetzal to take advantage of the country's limited natural resource potential.

After reading this historic sketch, many of you may be saying that if your itinerary includes a stop in Guatemala you will stay on board. I hope that would not be the case because as a tourist traveling in a group, you will be perfectly safe. Even if you use your free time in Antigua or at Lake Atitlan to walk around on your own, you will be well received by the locals and not be in any danger. The drug lords and their thugs do not target foreign tourists, especially in the major venues such as Antigua or in the national parks. So please enjoy your visit to Guatemala.

WHAT TO SEE: Puerto Quetzal offers the visitor absolutely nothing. This is simply a commercial port that provides anchorage for cruise ships. A rather nice passenger terminal has been built and there is an outdoor market area for the selling of traditional crafts and to enable dance performances when passengers disembark or in the afternoon when they begin returning. Thus it is vital to plan on participating in one of the ship's many tours. Guatemala is a beautiful country with a rich cultural tapestry, and it would be a shame to spend the day on board the ship rather than developing a feel for the land and its people. You can arrange on board for a private car and driver/guide or you will have the option of going on a group tour. In this particular instance, I recommend the group tour, as a coach filled with tourists is less likely to have any incident. Taxis are not a good idea even if they are available, which I do not recall seeing in Puerto Quetzal.

Each of the major destinations is discussed in detail in the remainder of this chapter, and I have a few recommendations with regard to shopping or dining for Antigua, Guatemala City and Lake Atitlan in the event any of you do decide upon a private car with a driver/guide. For visits to Tikal or Copan, charter flights are the only way to do a return trip in a single day, therefore those are organized group tours and lunch will be included. And there will be little time for shopping other than in whatever major shop is on the tour itinerary.

VISITING ANTIGUA: The colonial city of Antigua is the major cultural highlight of a visit by ship to Puerto Quetzal. The drive takes a bit over an hour, and the route takes the coach between two of the country's major active volcanic peaks - Fuego and Agua. Fuego is the more active, but a third peak called Acatenango will often puff out some dark clouds of ash. Agua may also be putting out some white plumes of steam on the same day. And then there is always the chance for a significant eruption of any of the three peaks. The drive is beautiful, and depending upon the volcanoes, it can sometimes be rather exciting when you see even a small eruption.

The city of Antigua sits in a round bowl flanked by these massive volcanic peaks. As the capital from 1541 to 1774, it developed magnificent architecture in the form of churches, government buildings and palatial homes. Even though the great 1773 earthquake destroyed much, many buildings did survive while others were restored. The city has always remained steeped in its historic charm and today with UNESCO World Heritage Status, it is thriving as a major tourist destination. There has also been a significant number of expatriate American and British retirees who have chosen Antigua, adding to the economic stability. An all day tour to Antigua is a wonderful way to learn about the richness of Guatemala's history and engage in a visual experience that is very memorable. Lunch is generally provided, and there are several outstanding many interesting sights that you will be taken to see.

Antigua is laid out in a grid with the central plaza being the focal hub. The main cathedral and the civic administrative palace are both located on the plaza. There are many smaller churches dotting the landscape. Inner Antigua contains the traditional adobe walled compounds where the residences face interior courtyards and have few windows facing outward to the street. Most of the streets are cobbled, and you will feel like you have entered a time warp. There is a definite sense of "magic" to the aura of Antigua, and it is a city where photographers cannot resist. If you wish to photograph native peoples, please ask or show them your camera first. And if they agree, a small tip is expected. If you have Guatemalan currency, a tip of 25 Quetzales would be equal to three U. S. dollars.

Shopping in Antigua is very good if you are looking for silver jewelry, Guatemalan jade and hand woven items. Both are popular among tourists, and the quality can be excellent if you compare goods. You will have limited free time for shopping, and if possible visit:

* Nim Po't Centro de Textiles Tradiciones - Located at Avenida 5a Norte #29. This is a major warehouse style shop that features outstanding woven ware and other Guatemalan crafts. Hopefully your tour bus may stop here. They currently are not posting any hours, but generally they are open when they know ship passengers will be coming to Antigua.

* The Original Jade Factory and Museum - This is often a designated tour stop. It is located in the town center at Avenida 4a Oriente #24. The jade demonstration and lecture are worth watching even if you do not make a purchase. They do not post any business hours, but when ships are in Puerto Quetzal, you can be sure they will be open because so many passengers come to Antigua.

* Colibre - At Avenida 4a Calle Oriente #38, this is another outstanding shop for traditional woven wares. They are open daily from 9 AM to 6 PM.

Lunch is generally served to groups at the Casa Santo Domingo, which is a beautiful colonial hotel inside of what was once a convent. The hotel is in part museum, as the old church and many of the early buildings have been maintained as an exhibit. There is also an arts and crafts shop in the hotel courtyard. Lunch is often a buffet, so make sure that hot dishes are still hot, and stay away from raw items such as salad. Remember this is a third world country and the level of sanitation is not up to western standards. Although this is an excellent establishment, caution is still advised.

VISITING GUATEMALA CITY : The capital is only about 30 minutes from Antigua, but none of the cruise lines offer a tour to the country's capital and the largest city in Central America. Guatemala City is rather chaotic and traffic makes sightseeing for a few hours very difficult, thus it is just not considered to be a viable option. If you have a car and driver/guide, I strongly urge you not to visit Guatemala City. Yes it is a very interesting major city of 2,110,000. But to do justice to visiting, you need at least two whole days, otherwise you will be simply attempting to see its major sights on a limited schedule without much success. Therefore I am not making any recommendations regarding shopping or dining venues.

VISITING LAGO DE ATITLÁN: This large and very deep lake fills an ancient volcanic caldera and is rimmed by towering volcanic peaks. Situated in the central highlands of Guatemala, Lake Atitlán is surrounded by numerous traditional villages where the local inhabitants are strongly Mayan in their cultural traditions. Without question, the lake and its villages produce the most photographed landscape in all of Guatemala. An all day coach journey to the lake combined with a motorized launch trip to the historic village of Panajachel enables you to savor both the natural and cultural flavors of the country.

Not every cruise line will offer this trip because given the distance and infrastructure involved, it is quite a costly outing. The five star cruise lines generally have this trip as an option. If you do happen to be on one of the five star ships and decide upon this tour, keep in mind that it involves about 2.5 hours of driving each way on relatively narrow roads. But you will be rewarded with incredible scenery and a chance to explore the living Mayan culture of the country. I will not offer any shopping or dining venues because such tours are totally planned and you will not have flexibility to make your own discoveries. As for going by private car with a driver/guide, I would recommend against it. The organized tour is better able to coordinate the motor launch and the afternoon meal along with the local guides.

VISITING TIKAL: One of the three greatest archaeological sites in the Western Hemisphere, Tikal is an ancient classic Maya city located in far northern Guatemala. Tikal became the center of administration for one of the largest and most powerful of the ancient Maya states, its grand buildings rising to impressive heights. Its largest temple rises over 46 meters or 150 vertical feet, reached by a very steep staircase. There are numerous temple pyramids and imposing buildings now reclaimed and restored, giving this site a grand appearance. The area has been designated a National Park and has received UNESCO World Heritage Site status.

Tikal's period of greatness lasted for around 200 years, and it is believed to have been conquered by the ancient city of Teotihuacan in the central valley of Mexico during the 5th century. The new rulers were ultimately absorbed culturally and the city continued to be a major center of power until sometime in the 9th century. Tikal is approximately two hours by charter plane from Puerto Quetzal, followed by another 20 to 30 minute drive from the airport to the National Park. You can figure on roughly five hours of travel time to Tikal and returning to the ship. This is an all day journey, and it is not recommended for anyone who is not in good physical condition. The climate of the Yucatan is tropical, which means hot and humid. The flight can often be a bit bumpy, especially flying over the central mountains where there are sharp up and down drafts, as jet aircraft are not used for these excursions.

Once at Tikal, you will be taken on a guided tour of the major highlights of the city. Without a guide, the ruins have little real meaning. They are simply spectacular and photogenic. But you need to understand the importance of Tikal and its influence upon the region. This can only be learned with the services of a guide.

Within the national park there is a gift shop that offers both souvenir type items and some native crafts produced locally. Actual artifacts of Pre Colombian origin are not legally sold, so beware of any outside vendors trying to con you into buying anything they call an artifact.

Lunch will be provided as part of the tour, and you will not have an opportunity to select the venue. Given the very hot and humid nature of the environment, be sure to eat only foods that were cooked and are being served fresh and hot. In these tropical environments it is quite easy to contract dysentery.

VOLCANO VISIT: A climb of Pacaya Volcano near Antigua can be quite an arduous, yet very exciting experience. Many cruise lines will have an organized tour to Pacaya that includes climbing the slopes of the volcano. This tour is dependent upon the level of activity of the mountain, as all guides are cognizant of the need to keep their guests safe. Normally on such a tour there is no lunch provided and there are no shopping venues close by unless the coach transporting you stops for any length of time in Antigua.

For those wanting to stay closer to Puerto Quetzal, some cruise lines will offer more localized tours to a nearby safari park or coffee plantation. These are short half-day tours that really do not give you any of the true cultural flavor of Guatemala.

* **Auto Safari Chapin:** The safari park gives animal lovers an opportunity to see much of the native wildlife of Guatemala in a natural surrounding. It is essentially a game reserve, but created as much to entertain and educate the visitor as to protect the wildlife.

* **Visiting a coffee plantation or Macadamia nut farm:** Many of the cruise lines offer a short trip to visit either a local coffee plantation or Macadamia nut farm to view how these two products are raised and processed for export

FINAL WORDS: One again I remind you that you should plan to attend one of the excursions because there is absolutely nothing for visitors to do in Puerto Quetzal, as it is strictly an industrial port. Guatemala may still be a country plagued by internal cultural strife, this time relating to the drug wars. But as a visitor, and in a group setting you will be perfectly safe. During any free time in Antigua, it is safe to go off on your own so long as you keep to the main streets. Hiring a private car and driver to visit Guatemala City is not something I would advise because the city is very congested and you will not find that it is as enjoyable a place to visit as Antigua.

On the historic streets of Antigua, Guatemala

A lazy afternoon in downtown Antigua

The local governmental palace in Antigua

One of the colorful marketplaces for Guatemalan crafts in Antigua

A steam eruption of Volcan Acatenango near Antigua

On the shores of magnificent Lago de Atitlan (Work of Francisco Anzola, CC BY SA 2.0, Wikimedia.org)

many villages surrounding Lago de Atitlan (Work of Murray Foubister, CC BY SA 2.0, Wikimedia.org)

The Acropolis at Tikal National Park (Work of Jose Rafael Luna Lop..., CC BY SA 3.0, Wikimedia.org)

MÉXICO AS A NATION

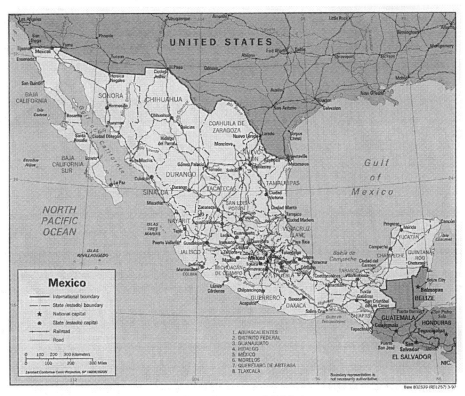

A locational map of México

México is the largest Latin American nation in North America in both land area and population. With 761,606 square miles it is the third largest Latin American nation in physical size after Brazil and Argentina. With 119,530,000 people, it is the second most populous nation in Latin America and it is one of the major powers of the Western Hemisphere. México is the most populous Spanish-speaking nation in the world, and it is a nation with a long and often turbulent history. To Americans and Canadians, México is a country that is familiar to millions because of its popularity as a tourist destination. The majority of North American visitors, however, tend to visit primarily the beach resorts that have developed an infrastructure catering to their tastes. People from the eastern states or provinces favor visiting the Yucatan Peninsula, enjoying such beaches as Cancun and Cosumel. For those living in the western states and provinces, it is the Pacific resorts that are most often patronized. Resorts such as Cabo San Lucas, Mazatlan, Puerto Vallarta and Ixtapa feature prominently. Up until the

141

1980's, the most favored beach resort was Acapulco, but it has lost its luster, as will be noted in the chapter devoted to the Acapulco port call. Fewer North Americans favor visiting cities in the interior, and that is a shame because the rich tapestry of Mexican history unfolded in the great cities of the central highlands. And it is here that one finds true Mexican heritage.

The news media has in recent years put quite a scare into North American visitors through their ongoing coverage of the drug cartels and the violence they have wrought to the country. There is no denying that such violence exists, and that the Mexican authorities have been hard pressed to gain the upper hand. Thousands of innocent people have been terrorized and/or killed in the last ten years in many regions of the country bordering the United States or where rival drug cartels have set up shop. But if you look closely at the statistics, it has been rare for innocent tourists to be caught up in these incidents. When traveling in México on your own, or even if you venture away from the ship on your own, here are the important tips that can make a difference between a safe visit and ending up becoming a victim:
* Never enter the poor barrios or market areas without being accompanied by a licensed guide.
* Never walk down dark or narrow streets on your own.
* Do not dress in an ostentatious manner when out in public.
* Do not wear expensive jewelry or watches.
* Keep your camera or handbag close to your body.
* Do not count out large sums of money in public.
* Only use reputable taxis that have been called for in advance from a hotel, restaurant or shop. It is not good to hail a taxi on the street.
* Do not walk alone at night.
* Having a working knowledge of Spanish is very helpful, especially in setting up an atmosphere of confidence when out on your own.

During the course of your ship's visit to México, unless you have traveled in the country before and feel comfortable, you are best off to take ship sponsored tours to maximize both your comfort and sightseeing.

PHYSICAL SETTING: A brief description of the physical components of the Mexican landscape are necessary to help set each port of call within its proper context relative to the rest of the nation. México is a large and diverse country, especially in its north to south latitudinal range. The country extends from the lower mid latitudes southward well into the tropics, thus giving it a diversity of climates and biospheres. México is also a very rugged country, having many major mountain ranges and high interior plateaus. And altitude also plays a major role in determining the climatic patterns and landscapes of any area, especially within the tropics. The Mexican Central Plateau, which straddles the Tropic of Cancer, has a mild climate and is home to the majority of the nation's population. On average, for every 1,000 foot rise in altitude, the air temperature will drop 5.5 degrees Fahrenheit on average.

There are five major ranges of mountains that dominate the majority of the country. These include:
* Baja California Peninsular Ranges - An extension of the coastal mountains of California, the mountains of the Baja Peninsula are relatively rugged, with a maximum elevation of 10,157 feet, but are relatively dry with little but scrub vegetation.
* Sierra Madre Occidental - The major range that parallels the Pacific coast of the mainland. The Sierra Madre are intensely rugged, containing the famous Barranca del Cobre, one of the world's greatest canyon complexes. The highest peak reaches 10,863 feet and these mountains contain beautiful forests of primarily pine.
* Sierra Madre Oriental - The major range that parallels the Gulf of México coastline with the highest peak reaching 12,139 feet and these mountains contain lush forests, with pine in the higher elevations and more tropical vegetation on lower slopes.
* Transverse Volcanic Range - This massive range of mountains runs from east to west along a plate boundary right through the middle of the country. The mountains are all of volcanic origin, with numerous active peaks. The most famous are the twin volcanoes of Popocatépetl at 17,887 feet, Iztaccihuatl at 17,343 feet and the country's highest mountain, Orizaba at 18,491 feet. These snowcapped giants are all potentially highly explosive, yet they are very close to densely populated cities.
* Sierra Madre del Sur - The southern mountains that begin south of the Transverse Volcanic Range and extend on into Central America. Their highest elevations reach 12,149 feet and even at this altitude in tropical latitudes snow is commonplace during winter.

143

The upper slopes do contain a mix of pine and broad leaf evergreen trees.

Between the Sierra Madre Occidental and Oriental is the great highland Plateau of México, a semi arid to humid grassland region that makes up the core of the nation. There are numerous sub plateaus as a result of smaller mountain ranges rising up within the greater plateau. And to the south there are highland regions between the Transverse Volcanic Range and the Sierra Madre del Sur. Most of the population of the nation lives in the highlands, as the coastal environments are hot and humid

The Yucatan Peninsula is a vast limestone plain with elevations just above sea level. The climate is a wet/dry tropical regime, and rainfall is collected in sinkholes, as there are no flowing rivers. The thick scrub forests make travel in this region very difficult, yet this was home to the great Maya civilization.

The northern parts of México are all arid to semi arid, depending upon location. The cold ocean currents of the Pacific Ocean help to create intense aridity on the Baja Peninsula and the northern coastal margins of the Gulf of California. Inland the land is semi arid, receiving between 10 and 15 inches of moisture with summer being the major rainy season. And on occasion, a Pacific hurricane may make landfall on the Baja Peninsula. The land is covered in scrub mesquite and grass whereas the Baja Peninsula and the northern reaches around the Gulf of California show a mix of cacti and hearty plants capable of withstanding the high heat of summer and a rainfall regime of less than 10 inches per year. The high mountains of the mainland are cloaked in forests of pine and oak.

The Gulf of México coastline is humid, cloaked in a mix of tropical trees and grasses. Rainfall peaks during summer, especially when the area is struck by occasional hurricanes. Yucatan is the most hurricane prone portion of the nation. The southern Pacific coastline from the Transverse Volcanic Range southward is also very warm and humid with a peak summer rainy season. This area is also prone to hurricanes that develop farther south off the coast of Panama.

All of México with the exception of the far northern border area with Arizona, New Mexico and Texas is subject to earthquake activity. The most intense earthquakes occur along the Baja Peninsula and through the heartland of the country along the Transverse Volcanic Range. The last catastrophic earthquake struck in Ciudad de México in 1984, killing close to 15,000. It had a magnitude on the Richter scale in excess of eight. Volcanic eruptions have not been too significant from the perspective of loss of life or property, but the potential is there. Pico de Colima, close to the Pacific coast is the most active major volcano, emitting great plumes of ash on a regular basis. In the late 1940's, a small volcanic cinder cone was born in a cornfield, witnessed by the farmer. This became the famous Paricutin Volcano that ultimately buried the local village in lava.

A BRIEF HISTORY: To cover the history of México would require a volume far larger than this traveler's companion. For the purpose of this book, the historic synopsis will be brief, but informative enough to enable you to appreciate each of the ports of call within the greater whole of the nation. It would do a disservice to my readers if I were to ignore the history since many of the excursions are directly tied to sites that are of historic significance.

The Pre-Columbian period of México alone could fill a volume. This land was the birthplace of several great civilizations that built one upon the other, and their technological and artistic accomplishments diffused outward to influence native tribes thousands of miles away. It is said that the central valleys in the highlands are the birthplace of farming for North America. The raising of maize, beans, squash, tomatoes, avocado and cacao were essential to the indigenous diet. And think of the impact these foods have had upon the world since having been taken back to Europe by the Spanish. In addition, native cotton, tobacco, wild turkey, honey from stingless honeybees and many species of fish figured prominently into the food matrix of the region.

Civilization has a long history in the highlands. There were several great civilizations that arose, flourished and then led into the next era generally through conquest. Names such as Olmec, Toltec and Aztec are familiar to anyone who has traveled in the central parts of the country, as ruins of these great nations are everywhere. And in the Yucatan Peninsula, the Maya were the great society that contributed to the overall advancement of science and technology in the greater whole of México and Guatemala.

European history begins with Hernán Cortéz landing on the Gulf Coast and marching his troops inland to ultimately capture the great Aztec capital of Tenochtitlan in 1519. Soon after conquest, a new capital arose on the very foundations of Aztec pyramids and temples - Ciudad de México, known to the rest of the world as Mexico City. Today the capital is the largest city in population in North America and among the ten largest urban centers in the world. It was from here that Spanish rule spread throughout the highlands, forcing native people into second class status and servitude while Spanish overlords became an elite ruling class. By 1600, Spanish rule extended as far north as what is now the United States when settlement was made along the upper Rio Grande at Santa Fe. Great mineral wealth in the form of gold, silver and copper flowed into Spanish hands and helped fuel the building of many magnificent cathedrals and governmental palaces, still gracing the landscape to the present day.

By 1821, the ordinary people reached the breaking point with Spanish rule and declared their independence, recognized as the Treaty of Córdoba. But the country then became mired in dictatorship after establishing a constitution. For three decades until the early 1850's, General Antonio López de Santa Ana rules with an iron hand. He invited Americans to help settle the frontiers of Texas, but after reversing policies toward them, he precipitated rebellion in which Texas became independent in 1836. But border conflicts drove the Texans to join the American Union, ultimately precipitating the Mexican American War of 1846 over the recognition of the Rio Grande as the border between the two nations. The end of the war in 1848 under the treaty of Guadalupe Hidalgo ceded more than half of the northern land area to the United States, including the riches of California.

When Santa Ana was defeated in 1854, the country had a succession of leaders, but all of them unable to govern successfully. Debt incurred by Santa Ana led México to later governments borrowing heavily from France, which in 1862 prompted an armed invasion of the country to exact reparations. It was also in part the result of conservative forces wanting to establish a monarchy in which the upper classes would still hold great power, as in the Spanish colonial era. The first popularly elected president Benito Juárez fled to the far north where his supporters waged guerrilla warfare until they were able to overthrow the French in 1867, capturing the pretender Emperor Maximilian and executing him. Benito Juárez was restored to power, and to this day he is celebrated as the father of modern México.

After Juárez died, nobody could match his hold on the spirit of the people, and the country was plunged into dictatorship under Porfirio Diaz whose rule despite being despotic did bring about economic stability and foreign investment. However, despite economic gains, the majority of the people did not benefit, and ultimately the hand of Diaz became so heavy that people rebelled. The Mexican Revolution that began in 1911, after another fraudulent election. The Revolution was quite brutal, and among the various revolutionary leaders, Pancho Villa became the most famous to Americans because of his daring raid for munitions across the border at Columbus, New Mexico. The American General Pershing chased Pancho Villa deep into the northern interior, but to no avail. In México he is seen as a great folk hero. Another revolutionary leader immortalized in a Hollywood movie was Emiliano Zapata. But lesser known to North Americans are the names of Alvaro Obregón and Francisco Madero, both later serving a term as president of the nation.

By 1928, many of the large landed estates were broken up and given to groups of peasant farmers under what became known as the ejido system. And by 1929, one political movement, Partido Revolucionario Institucional (PRI) emerged as the dominant political party, controlling the government until the election of 2000. During the World War II period, México supplied the United States with valuable minerals and farm laborers under a guest worker program. This helped stabilize the Mexican economy, but still the nagging problem of rural poverty continued, especially with rapid increases in population resulting from better health care. By the late 20th century, a combination of over population, governmental corruption and a growing trend toward drug violence encouraged more illegal immigration to the United States. This problem was exacerbated by the fact that the guest worker program had been drastically scaled back relative to the needs of the Mexican population. The introduction of NAFTA, the North American Free Trade Agreement brought more industrialization to northern México with the creation of large assembly plants called maquilladoras to take advantage of less costly labor. But this trend did not stem the flow of immigrants northward. And drug violence has reached an all time high, especially in border areas.

The rule of PRI ended in 2000 with the election of Vicente Fox of the opposition party known by its initials of PAN, Partido Acción Nacional. But 12 years of their rule did not bring great improvements, especially in the war against drugs. In 2012, PRI came back to power with its charismatic leader Enrique Peña Nieto, a handsome young man who has pledged to bring about sweeping changes. Only time will tell.

MEXICAN POTENTIAL: The country has great potential if it can reign in government corruption and the drug cartels. México is potentially a wealthy nation, rich in raw materials including oil, and with a large, urban population and a growing well-educated middle class. Tourism has been drastically hurt in recent years because of drug violence, and that is a major setback because of the role tourism has played in the economy. Hopefully the new administration can turn around the economy and make life better for the poor, which would in turn greatly reduce or even eliminate the illegal immigration problem.

Presidente Enrique Peña Nieto, elected in 2012 (Work of Presidencia Mx2012-2018

PUERTO CHIAPAS, CHIAPAS

Puerto Chiapas is a very new stop and only a few of the major cruise lines are at present including it on their itineraries. It is a specially constructed port for cruise ships, built to encourage visitors to the southernmost state of Chiapas, which borders Guatemala. Chiapas is probably the least known state among foreign visitors because of its remoteness from the rest of the country. And it has been a state beset by social and political upheaval throughout the late 20th century and into the present because of agitation from its predominantly native and mestizo population that has for over a century felt left out of Mexican political affairs and neglected when it comes to infrastructure development. Puerto Chiapas is part of a program to correct the neglect and focus upon tourism as one means of improving the economy.

Chiapas is a beautiful state with high volcanic mountains that are in effect an extension northward of the Guatemalan landscape. The coastal region was thickly covered in tropical rainforest vegetation, but much of the rainforest has been destroyed to expand both agriculture and ranching. Bananas are the important cash crop presently grown. The upland valleys between the high mountains are the favored climate, and it is here that most towns and villages are located, as is true in Guatemala. In the northern part of the state, the mountains give way to the southern margins of the Yucatan Peninsula, and it is here that the ancient Maya culture also existed as the southernmost part of that great empire. The most famous of the ruins are found at Palenque, comparable in many ways to Tikal.

BRIEF HISTORIC SKETCH: Of all 31 states and the Federal District of México Chiapas has the highest percentage of native peoples and mestizo, thus making it a region that always fell under the political heels of the government located far to the north in the great Central Valley of México. In essence, Chiapas has always been perceived of as backward and less worthy of inclusion. And through the centuries, the people of Chiapas have resisted government officials and troops, rising up in arms on numerous occasions. Subjugation and rebellion are two themes that describe Chiapas.

The mid 20th century was the most critical for Chiapas, as large numbers of refugees from political violence in Nicaragua, El Salvador and Guatemala flooded into Chiapas. At the same time, the Bishop of the Diocese of Chiapas attempted to organize the various native tribal groups, which also received support from leftist leaning groups. Ultimately all of the unrest culminated in 1994 when the Zapatistas captured several communities within Chiapas and raided local military establishments, gaining arms and munitions. Despite armed conflicts, the central authorities have attempted to pacify the region by pouring in economic aid and establishing programs to better the lives of the people. However, the Zapatista movement is still alive and the government cannot seem to find a common ground with what they represent and what it believes a state should show by way of loyalty to central authority. But at present, there is sufficient calm in Chiapas that tourism is developing and adding to the economy.

PUERTO CHIAPAS: This newly constructed cruise port is located on the edge of Puerto de San Benito, only 13 miles north of the border with Guatemala. The coastal region here is connected by one main highway to Tapachula in the interior, and it is here that there is regular scheduled airline service. The initial port development was undertaken in 1975 for both fishing and shipping of agricultural produce, in particular bananas. The cruise port opened in 2005.

To be very frank, there is absolutely nothing to do or see in Puerto Chiapas. There is a small beach area, but facilities are minimal and the neighboring small residential community offers no amenities for visitors. The nearest city of any size is Tapachula, located inland under the shadow of Tacaná Volcano, presenting a beautiful backdrop. Tapachula has around 300,000 residents but it is primarily a local trade center and also the official entry port for traffic incoming from Guatemala, a few miles to the east. As a border city, Tapachula has problems with drug violence, illegal Guatemalan and Salvadoran immigrants crossing northward, most en route to the United States. Prior to the 19th century this was a very small community, therefore its number of historic buildings is quite limited. So once again there is very little here to entice visitors who have come off the cruise ship.

WHAT TO SEE AND DO: The only way to make the day worthwhile is to sign up for one of the tours being offered by your cruise line. There is a lack of sufficient private cars with driver/guides, and local taxis are most unreliable and not the safest way to tour about. So if you are not one who is fond of group tours, this is one port where you really have no choice. Otherwise there is absolutely nothing to see or do since the port offers only a small gift shop and there is a public craft area for vendors right at the port entrance.

The tours I recommend are as follows, and will vary in their specifics according to each cruise line:

* Tapachula - Touring the city is somewhat interesting, as it is typical of the urban development of the state. Although not a very old city, it does give you the overall flavor of southern México, and with the volcanic backdrop, it does have some picturesque qualities. Within Tapachula the Saint Augustine Church and the Soconusco Archaeological Museum are of definite interest.

* Izapa Ruins - This set o ruins represents both Mayan and Olmec cultures. This gives you a chance to see the quality of construction of a Maya city without taking a flight to Palenque or Tikal. It is located at the base of Tacaná Volcano in a rather beautiful rainforest setting.

* Palenque - This would be an all-day tour with a flight from Tapachula by chartered plane to Palenque, which is across the mountain rib of the state and situated in the southern Yucatan Peninsula. It is most likely your cruise line will not offer this relatively expensive tour, as it is generally the five-star cruise lines that will provide such opportunities. But if a tour to Palenque is available, I would strongly recommend it unless you had previously been to Tikal.

* Coffee Plantation. - Located into the Sierra Madre de Sul Mountains, about a two hour drive from the ship, you enter the region of coffee plantations. And around the town of Argovia, there are tours offered whereby you visit a coffee plantation and see how the daily cup comes to be.

* Tuxtla Chico - A nearby town that is home to the processing of cacao grown in the area into chocolate. México has several regions where cacao is grown, and the production of chocolate is a long-standing tradition. You will have an opportunity to buy chocolate, generally cut into bricks that can be used for baking. Most Mexican chocolate contains cinnamon and is of excellent quality.

* A Mangrove Tour - Along the coast around Puerto Chiapas there are mangrove swamps that serve as home to numerous types of sea birds. Several of the cruise lines offer a boat tour through one of the mangroves. This is a short tour for those who do not want to spend half or a whole day traveling into the interior.

DINING OUT: On an all day tour to Palenque, lunch will be provided and you will not have any choice as to venues. None of the other tours are of sufficient length to offer lunch.

* If your tour to Tapachula does allow sufficient private time, the only lunch venue I would recommend is La Jefa Botanerico Rustico Mexicano, located at 1a Avenida Norte Esquina, this traditional Mexican restaurant offers very good food in a clean and nice setting. But remember to eat only cooked food and if you order a soft drink, make sure there are no ice cubes in it. Open Noon to 8 PM daily.

I would not recommend any restaurants in the port area. Puerto Chiapas is just starting to develop and it is not that well visited. Thus eating locally could cause you problems later with regard to severe intestinal upset. It is just not worth taking that chance.

SHOPPING: There are no specific shopping venues that I feel comfortable recommending. You will find that local crafts are similar to those created in Guatemala, but most tours will not afford you much time for shopping other than the tour to Tapachula. You will find both street vendors and small shops in Tapachula if given time to visit the central area.

FINAL WORD: Puerto Chiapas has a long way to go before its regional infrastructure can handle a greater variety of offerings. But what is presently offered is diverse enough to appeal to most tastes. You must keep in mind that you are visiting what is still considered to be a cultural backwater in México.

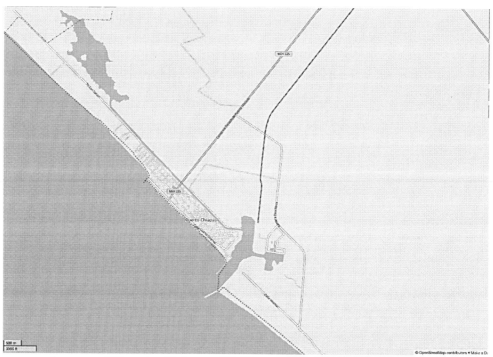

A map of Puerto Chiapas (© OpenStreetMap contributors)

Silversea's Silver Spirit in Puerto Chiapas (Work of Apimadero CC BY SA 3.0, Wikimedia.org)

The spectacular ruins of Palenque (Work of Liss 4567, CC BY SA 3.0, Wikimedia.org)

The ruins of Izapa (Work of Lorena Gutíerez G, CC BY SA 3.0, Wikimedia.org)

The House of Culture in Tapachula (Work of Alejandro Beristaín, CC BY SA 3.0, Wikimedia.org)

ACAPULCO, GUERRERO

Acapulco is the largest coastal city in México with a population of 1,021,000 in its metropolitan area. At one time during the first half of the 20th century, this was the grand beach resort of the entire nation, a city of great glamour and wealth. But during the last half of the 20th century with the rise of newer, less crowded coastal resorts on both the Pacific and Caribbean shores, Acapulco has seen a great decline in its position as the crown jewel of the Mexican shores. The massive influx of poor peasants from surrounding rural areas, the infiltration of the drug cartels and the congestion of its narrow coastal fringe combined to make Acapulco far less desirable than Cancun, Ixtapa, Puerto Vallarta and Cabo San Lucas. Today it caters as much to weekend visitors from the national capital and other major interior cities as it does to North American visitors. Because of its population, it does have excellent air services to many major cities in both North America and Europe, thus still attracting a fair share of the market, but nowhere near what it once did. Many Mexican scholars refer to Acapulco as a "faded grand damme."

In recent years the majority of cruise lines often bypass Acapulco because of the amount of drug violence that has taken place there. Passengers have not felt safe and as a result they often remain on board rather than even venturing out on shore excursions. But for the benefit of those cruise lines that are still offering Acapulco as a port of call, this chapter will give you a frank observation of the city, pointing out both the good and the undesirable aspects of spending a day in this major urban center.

THE SETTING: The main heart of Acapulco wraps around crescent shaped Acapulco Bay, backed up by steep mountains that encompass the entire city, coming down to the ocean both east and west of the city with steep cliffs. The newest parts of the city to be developing lies beyond the mountains to the northeast of the bay and to the east along a flat coastal plain where there is plenty of room for growth. The poorer neighborhoods cling to the hillsides behind the bay, as is typical in Latin American cities. Unlike Anglo America, hillsides are often the home to the poor unless they happen to be right adjacent to the sea. The wealthiest districts of Acapulco overlook the bay and the ocean coastline from the hills and cliffs that border both the western and eastern ends

157

of the bay, making this a choice area for development while the lower hillsides around the interior of the bay house the barrios. Beyond the ring of mountains is a sprawling area of new development, primarily housing lower and middle-income families, but unfortunately still developing in a piecemeal manner with few paved streets or sidewalks. Hundreds of thousands of people live in these rather unattractive new areas totally removed from the coastline. In this part of the city, which is now quite extensive, you would never know you are in a major coastal port since the mountains hide the ocean from view.

The climate of Acapulco is tropical, but with a distinct wet and dry regime. The winter months, which are prime tourist season, tend to be relatively dry. Temperatures average in the low to mid 80's and humidity is in a comfortable range. The summer months are slightly warmer, but much more humid with heavy thundershowers in the late afternoon. With a poorly developed infrastructure in the foothill suburbs, avalanches, mud slides and washed out streets or homes is rather commonplace. And when the occasional hurricane strikes, the debris from the hillsides can wash all the way down to the more expensive beachfront property, literally causing havoc.

The old city core or downtown caters primarily to the lower and middle-income community. Its streets are choked with traffic. The buildings are old, yet not historic and there is an air of decrepitude, making this a non-attractive zone for visitors. It is also an area where foreign visitors can become victims of petty street crime. But stretching from the old core along the bay is the grand cornice known as Avenida Costera Miguel Alemán. It is lined with high-rise hotels, apartments and condos. It is also the principal shopping street for visitors. Many high-end shops with famous brand names line the cornice, and there are many restaurants and nightclubs lining the street, making this the focal point for foreigners. And behind the cornice is the grand beach that has become so much a part of the Acapulco scene. Hotels and residences cannot lay claim to the beachfront, thus giving everyone access. This leads to the one harassing feature of the Acapulco beach - the myriad of vendors peddling everything from sunscreen to food to clothing and souvenirs. And they are as pesky as proverbial flies.

Overlooking both the eastern and western ends of the bay are the older, wealthy suburbs. The Las Playas Peninsula protrudes down into the bay, guarding the western entrance. It is here that many of the mid 20th century homes of film stars and other celebrity figures are located. At the northern end of the peninsula is the Hotel Mirador Acapulco. It overlooks a small cove on the Pacific coast where the high cliffs have become famous for the young men who dive into the churning waters of the cove as a means of performance for guests.

Ad of course if you watch from the hotel terrace, one of the representatives will come around asking for a donation for the divers, which is of course well deserved.

The eastern headlands guarding the bay have a commanding view of the whole city. And it is in these hills that several famous hotels have been built during the mid 20th century. The Las Brisas Acapulco is the most noted, its pink buildings being a predominant landmark. From here the main highway rounds the bay and then runs high above Puerto Marques Bay, a newly developing area, growing out of an old fishing village. Once out on the flat coastal plane, the main highway enters the Zona Diamante, the newest addition to the city. The most elegant and noted beachfront hotel is the Fairmont Acapulco Princess, the city's jewel in the crown of hotel properties. The remainder of this flat plain presents a mix of shopping malls, small hotels, apartments and condominiums in a rather unplanned manner.

ACAPULCO'S FASCINATING HISTORY: To understand this major city that has until recently been on every itinerary for ships making the Panama Canal transit between the American east and west coasts, it is first important to briefly review the history of Acapulco. Unlike the new beach resorts, this is a city with a long history as a major port for the country dating back to Spanish colonial times.

Long before the Spanish came, the Olmec, Maya and Aztec had influenced the area. The Aztec actually built a small outpost city just north of present day Acapulco, an excavation that is a current shore excursion for one of the major cruise lines. Acapulco dates to either 1523 or 1526, depending upon which historical reference one uses. The site was either explored from overland by one of Hernán Cortéz's officers or it was scouted from the sea, also authorized by Cortéz.

By 1531, the small port of Acapulco was established and had a road link to the capital. What put the city on the map was the development of a trade route to the Spanish Philippines. The annual Manila-Acapulco route would bring silks, spices and other luxury goods from the Philippines in exchange for Mexican gold. This trade lasted until just before the Mexican Revolution of 1821. To protect the route from English and Dutch marauders, the Fuerte San Diego was built, as the trade had brought many wealthy Spanish families to settle on Acapulco Bay.

Despite the presence of the fort, the Dutch did attack in 1615, and the fort was later destroyed by an earthquake in 1776, but soon rebuilt. It still stands today opposite the cruise ship terminal and affords good views over the heart of the city. During the Mexican Revolution, the city was attacked and much of it burned down. It was the revolution that ended the Manila-Acapulco galleon traffic. But soon the city became an important provisioning stop on the route from Panama or around South America to San Francisco during the gold rush era.

The popularity of Acapulco as an international resort was given a massive boost when Edward, Prince of Wales visited in 1920 and was captivated by the beauty of the bay. On his recommendation, many of Europe's nobility and royals ventured to Acapulco, and at the same time the Hollywood royals began to vacation here. This patronage lasted well into the 1970's, but it became augmented by less expensive flights and hotels once jet travel became commonplace. The end result was to turn Acapulco into a resort for the greater masses, and this discouraged the more elite visitors who began to look for less accessible venues. What brought Mexican tourists was the completion in the 1990's of the Ruta del Sol, the toll highway from México City to Acapulco that now enables people to come en mass for weekend getaways.

Unfortunately since 2000, Acapulco has become the major way station on the route from Bolivia and Colombia for drugs heading north into the United States. Rival drug cartels have been battling it out for control of the state of Guerrero in which Acapulco is the major city. There have been several shootouts between drug gangs and the police, and many brutal atrocities committed in the past few years. The police maintain a strong presence, especially along the cornice and in the old downtown, but as late as 2011, there was a major shootout in front of the cruise ship terminal. I could go on, but there is no point in belaboring the fact that Acapulco has become a violent city in which atrocities have been committed not only between the drug gangs and police, but politicians and foreign tourists have also been caught up in many such events.

The question you are no doubt asking now is whether it is safe to leave the ship. And the answer is a qualified yes. But to play safe, only go out while on an excursion offered by your cruise line. I do not recommend walking the streets of Acapulco on your own. I have done so in 2010 and 2011, no doubt foolishly, but speaking the language I somehow did not feel unsafe. But these thugs who are the cause of the problems do not ask if you speak English or Spanish. So I would not go off on my own today. And it is this situation that is hurting Acapulco and causing greater numbers of visitors to seek their fun in the sun at other resorts along the coasts. Even if you go on an organized tour, I would recommend that you do not wear any expensive watches or jewelry, and do not take a lot of cash with you. When out in public simply take the normal precautions you would in many major cities with regard to pickpockets. And do not stray away from the group. If given any free time along the heart of the cornice where there is a lot of foot traffic, then it is totally safe go walking on your own. And the same holds true on the grounds of the Fairmont Princess Hotel.

WHAT TO SEE: So long as you take one of your ship's tours, you will enjoy the sights of Acapulco. Or you will also be quite safe if you arrange for a private car with a driver/guide. But do not use local taxis, as they can be unreliable and also their driving habits leave a lot to be desired. Despite all that has been said about the city's violent history, there are still places of interest for the visitor. Depending upon which tour you choose, there are many interesting sights that are worthy of your time. These include:

* The Divers at the Hotel Mirador Acapulco in La Quebrada - The young men who dive with no safety equipment, plunging into the swirling water below cliffs that are nearly 200 feet high exhibit a level of daring that is quite a performance. This has been a classic sight since the early 20th century.

* Driving the Costera Miguel Alemán - Here you have a chance to see the extent of the hotel, apartment and condo development that has created quite a wall of high-rises along the main waterfront of the city. You can then picture what this strip was like back 30 years ago during the height of the city's grand era.

* Zona Diamante _ A visit to the Zona Diamante shows you the effort being put into trying to recapture the grandeur of old Acapulco. The drive out to this new area always includes a walking visit through the magnificent grounds of the Fairmont Princess Acapulco Hotel.

* Fuerte San Diego - This ancient fort overlooks the cornice and has excellent views of the waterfront. It is also the most historic building complex, dating back to the early Spanish colonial era. Within the fort is the Historical Museum of Acapulco. Open 9 AM to 6 PM daily.

* Cathedral of Acapulco - Located in the downtown of the Old City, this is actually a 20th century cathedral and built in a non-traditional form, but still has a striking quality. Do not go here unless it is part of your tour or you go with a private guide.

* Tehuacalco - A new national park located about 90 minutes via the main highway north into the lower Sierra Madre del Sur. Tehuacalco is a small Aztec community recently excavated and very worthwhile for anyone who is interested in pre-Colombian cultures. Not all cruise lines offer this excursion, but if yours does and you are interested in Aztec culture, it is a worthy expedition.

DINING OUT: On a one-day cruise or even if your ship stays overnight, as some do, you will be best off dining on board the ship. As noted, taxis are not reliable in any Mexican city. If, however, you were staying in a hotel, the concierge would have a list of taxi drivers they trust and they prearrange pick up and drop off time. But to just take a taxi from the cruise terminal is not very safe, especially after dark. There are no quality restaurants within walking distance of the cruise terminal. All of the really fine restaurants are either located in the Costa Azul or the Zona Diamante, which is just too far from the ship to reach. If you happen to have a private car and driver/guide then many of these establishments are accessible. In that event, ask the local representative that comes on board the ship or that is located within the cruise terminal or your driver/guide for recommendations that will satisfy your specific tastes at either lunch or dinner. Some cruise lines offer all day tours that will include lunch, and the restaurants they choose are required to meet a higher level of quality and sanitation. If you are on one of the up market cruise lines and lunch is offered on a tour, you can be sure it will be at a very fine local restaurant.

SHOPPING: Many visitors to Acapulco look forward to shopping in the heart of the modern city along the Costera. There are hundreds of high end shops selling sportswear, bathing suits, jewelry and evening ware along with perfumes and colognes. There are also nice men's clothing as well. But much of what you can buy here is also available at high-end shops in your home city as well. Many people do believe that there are good bargains in cologne and jewelry because of little or no excise or import tax. But you need to be ware that less reputable shops often cut perfume to water it down, and jewelry is not always what it appears to be. In the area of arts and crafts, there are both reputable upmarket shops that sell quality craft items and then there is a combination of street vendors and the public marketplace. However, the marketplace is in Old Acapulco and you should only go in the company of a reputable guide. It is an enjoyable experience to bargain in the local market, but unless you are accompanied by a guide, you are stepping into a less savory part of the city.

Here are my recommendations as to a few major shops in the genre of handcrafts:
* Mercado de Artesanias - Located at Avenida Cinco de Mayo in Old Acapulco, this is the best place to buy traditional Mexican handcrafts. And most of the shop and stall owners expect you to bargain on the price. It is part of the whole act of buying. However, do not walk to this marketplace on your own. You need to be in the company of a reputable guide. Open 9 AM to 6 PM daily.
* Mercado Municipal - Located at Calle Diego Hurtado de Mendoza and Avenida Constituyentes - This is a large flea market indoors that is comprised of many individual vendors. They sell everything from "junk" to good quality. You need to have a guide with you first of all to go to this part of the city and secondly to help you make wise purchases. Open 6 AM to 6 PM daily.
* Casa de la Cultura - Located at Avenida Costera Miguel Aleman # 4834, in the main shopping area, this small shop does offer high quality arts and crafts of traditional origin. But without a car and driver, it is difficult to reach this shop on your own. Open 9 AM to 9 PM daily.

As for the fancy shopping malls and "glitzy" hotel shops, I will not make any recommendations, as they are too numerous. But I will state that most of what they sell is overpriced, similar to the hotel shops in Las Vegas.

FINAL WORDS: I trust that all of my warnings about being careful in Acapulco do not cause you to simply remain on board the ship. It is worth taking at least one half-day tour at a minimum simply to see this massive and crowded city that has such a famous image. It is still a worthy place to at least get an overview of at the very least. But unfortunately in good faith I cannot recommend that you just get out there and walk and explore since this does carry an inherent risk. Yes I have done it over the years, but after my last two visits, I have come to realize that it is just not the safest thing to do. If you are staying in one of the major hotels along the costera or out in the Zona Diamante, then you have local venues in which to feel safe walking. But unfortunately the cruise terminal is on the edge of Old Acapulco. The last time I was there, a string of shootings had taken place a few days before. The police were out in the area near the cruise terminal, patrolling in their armored personnel carriers, carrying rifles and machine guns and wearing black face masks to prevent them from being identified by any potential drug gang members. It was unnerving to say the least. There are periods of calm between the outbreaks of violence, so you must inquire from the local representatives that come on board as to the conditions for getting out on your own. Group motor coach tours are always safe when booked through the cruise line, so do not be alarmed by what I have written. I would just be remiss if I did not mention the lurking potential for violence. This is a major city as well as a popular tourist destination, and thus it has experienced its fair share of criminal activity.

But if conditions are unfavorable for private sightseeing, then by all means book a tour so that at least you see something of Acapulco. It is a great city even though its glory days are long since passed.

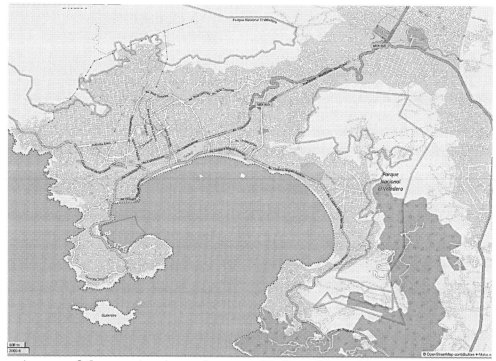

A map of the greater Acapulco area (© OpenStreetMap contributors)

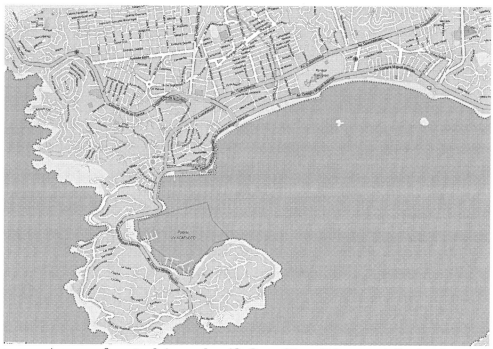

A map of central Acapulco (© OpenStreetMap contributors)

Along the Malecón below Fuerte San Diego, view to northwest

Looking down on the heart of the tourist zone to the northeast

The poor districts climbing the hillsides behind the Malecón

Older expensive homes on Manzanillo Bay on the west side

In the heart of Old Acapulco's downtown area where tourists do not venture

Much of the old inner city is too risky for visitors

East along the Malecón in the heart of the tourist area

Tourist oriented shops and restaurants along the Malecón

High rise hotels and condominiums along the Malecón

The western Malecón toward La Quebrada

Cliff divers at La Quebrada

Wealthy homes on hillsides opposite the city on the east side of the bay

Acapulco Princess Hotel in the Zona Diamante

The new Tehuacalco National Park inland from Acapulco

The ancient Aztec ball court at Tehuacalco

The ancient remains of the governor's palace at Tehuacalco

IXTAPA/ZIHUATANEJO, GUERRERO

Located a few hundred miles farther northwest along the coast of the state of Guerrero, the twin cities of Ixtapa and Zihuatanejo have become a very popular tourist venue. Unlike Acapulco, these are small urban centers with a combined population of only 113,000 residents. Being somewhat isolated from the mainstream of the country, this is an area that has not seen any drug violence since the first decade of the 21st century thanks to strong military intervention. In recent years the area has been relatively safe, except for occasional kidnappings of wealthier Mexican citizens. It is also a relatively prosperous community with significant employment, and thus street crime against visitors is minimal. Not all of the major cruise lines stop here, but for those who do, guests are exposed to a more placid and genuine side to life in México.

THE LANDSCAPE: The twin towns are separated by a low set of hills, but it is Zihuatanejo that is the far older and historic of the two. It is also built around a very deep harbor, but one that has very swift undercurrents. There is a dock that is capable of handling a single cruise ship, but it would be rare for two to be scheduled for the same day. Some cruise companies, however, do prefer to anchor in the bay and tender their passengers onshore.

The countryside is one of low hills that extend inland to meet the foothills of the higher Sierra Madre del Sur, the chain that runs south from the transverse range, and it extends on into Guatemala. Ixtapa is built on a more open bay that does not provide anchorage for ships. Ixtapa is a new, planned beach resort and it has absolutely no docking facilities let alone acceptable anchorage. It is separated from Zihuatanejo by a few miles of hills, linked by one major highway. And unlike its neighbor, Ixtapa is a 20th century creation.

The landscape is one of tropical wet/dry forest, being subjected to two distinct seasons with summer having the heaviest rainfall. The temperatures are in the 80's for much of the year, rising slightly along with the humidity during the summer months, as the latitude is still well within the tropics. But cooling breezes do blow in off the Pacific, moderating the climate.

There are several small fishing villages dotting the shoreline both north and south of the two cities, some of these towns being quite pleasant for tourists to visit, as this is a relatively safe area in which drug violence has not been a problem. And the local police understand the value of keeping tourists safe because they comprise a major portion of the local economy.

HISTORY OF SETTLEMENT: The earliest explorations of the area date to the 1520's when the Spanish were searching for gold throughout the country. After discovering the bay at Zihuatanejo, the Spanish built two ships to sail to the Philippines, but one ship was lost and the second never returned to Spain after arriving. Ultimately it was Acapulco that became the primary port for trade with Manila, as noted in the prior chapter.

Settlement in the region was minimal. Ixtapa was awarded as an encomienda, but there were few natives in the area to be impressed into service, thus it was Spanish peasants who worked the land, raising cotton, cacao and maize. And lumbering was done, with hardwoods such as oak and walnut being cut. Zihuatanejo developed as a minor fishing port and supply center for the few haciendas that existed in the hinterland. But essentially the area was considered to be a backwater.

During the revolution against Spain, this area was uninvolved. But during the 1911 war to free the country from the rule of Porfirio Díaz, the people of Zihuatanejo did join in the fighting, and thus incurred some government reprisals. Into the first half of the 20th century, this area still remained on the fringe of development, as the country began to modernize.

It was the government that brought vitality and attention to the area when it decided to develop the former encomienda into a tourist resort. With money from the Bank of México, secured by a loan from the World Bank, the master plan was developed for Ixtapa. Thus the resort is a totally planned community with all of its streets and land uses predetermined. The other resort that the government planned and developed at the same time was Cancún on the Caribbean coast. Ixtapa has been successful, but it has never been able to compete with the dynamic development of Puerto Vallarta farther north along the coast.

WHAT TO SEE AND DO: Depending upon the cruise line you are on, the number and diversity of excursions will vary. Most cruise lines do have a half-day coach tour around Zihuatanejo and then over to Ixtapa where passengers have an opportunity to walk along the beach, visit the hotels and shops and simply have a relaxing time. Tours into the surrounding countryside are few in number, as there are no famous historic sites. The local fishing villages are sometimes visited on a separate half-day tour along with a stop to visit a cocoa or other tropical plantation.

For a full day's tour, one cruise line does offer the opportunity to sail to Playa Manzanillo where one can enjoy snorkeling and swimming in the crystal clear waters.

Most people simply spend part or all of their day enjoying the quiet charm of the waterfront and central business area of Zihuatanejo, absorbing some of the local color and savoring some genuine Mexican cuisine. The city center extends back several blocks from the Paseo del Pescador, or fisherman's path, which follows the curvature of the bay. It is lined with quaint cafes and cantinas, affording one the atmosphere that would be expected in a Mexican fishing town.

The only important site of note is:
* El Museo Arqueológico de la Costa Grande - Located at the south end of the Paseo de los Pescadores, has many artifacts representing history and archaeology of not only the Guerrero region, but from as far away as ancient Aztec, Toltec and Olmec civilizations. It also has many artifacts from the Spanish colonial period. It is open daily from 9 AM to 5 PM.

DINING OUT: The cafes in Zihuatanejo do offer very fresh seafood at reasonable prices. In choosing a cafe for lunch, people must judge as to their comfort level. The majority are very clean, but it is still recommended that you do not eat any raw vegetables or drink any beverages containing ice because of possible bacterial contamination. This is always a wise precaution.

There are a few dining venues in Zihuatanejo within walking distance from the ship tender dock that I do comfortably recommend:
* Carmelita's Cafe - Located on Avenida Morelos just north of Calle Heroico Colegio Militar about one mile northeast of where the ship tenders dock. It is open from 8 AM to 4 PM, serving breakfast and lunch. This is a popular local establishment that receives rave reviews. It serves very traditional and genuine Mexican cuisine with a local twist.
* La Terracita - Located in town at Calle Adelita # 6, about 3/4 mile from the town center and open from 8 AM to Noon and then again from 6 to 10 PM. You can have a late traditional Mexican breakfast, or if your ship is staying into the evening, you can have dinner. But they do not serve lunch. Their menu is very traditional and genuine and the quality is excellent.

DINING OUT IN IXTAPA: Unfortunately your standard coach tour to Ixtapa leaves you with a maximum of 30 minutes free time, not enough to have a leisurely meal in one of the local restaurants. Taking a taxi from Zihuatenejo is not something I would recommend, as I generally am reluctant to do so anywhere in the country. Only when you are staying in a four or five-star hotel where they have arrangements with the most reputable taxi companies is using a taxi advisable.

SHOPPING: The central downtown core is filled with shops that serve local needs, but there are also many that sell local arts and crafts items, catering to visitors in a variety of price ranges. And of course in México you are expected to bargain as to price. Never accept the listed price on any item when in a shop selling primarily to visitors. If you are buying necessities, for example in a pharmacy, the norm is to accept the price that is on the item. There is a crafts market in Zihuatanejo, and here you will find a variety of items from all parts of the country. México is noted for its ceramics, lacquer wares, weavings and woodcarvings. There are no shops of any special note, as most tend to sell the same craft items you will see anywhere in the tourist oriented ports along the west coast.

SHOPPING IN IXTAPA: If your cruise line allows you some free time on a tour to Ixtapa, you will find that the shops here are more oriented toward clothing for the beach and general resort living. There are no specific shops to recommend.

FINAL NOTES: Although this may not be a dynamic port of call, you will find that a day spent in Zihuatanejo with a couple of hours over in Ixtapa presents you with relaxing chance to enjoy the more serene aspects of Mexican culture in contrast to the frenetic activity of the major beach resorts. If you are cruising north, then the next two stops in Puerto Vallarta and Cabo San Lucas will be filled with much activity. Some cruise itineraries may include Manzanillo, but this is also a very relaxed stop similar to Zihuatanejo. And if your cruise is southbound, this stop will give you a chance to unwind and relax after the two prior busy ports of call.

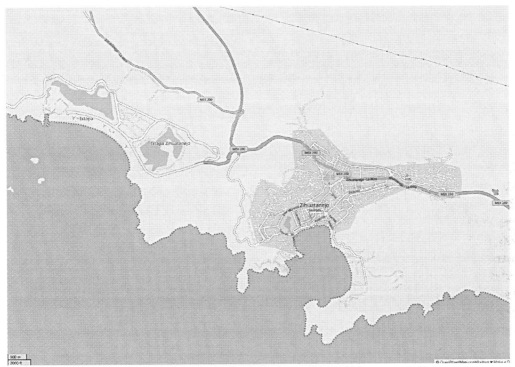

A map of Ixtapa/Zihuatanejo (© OpenStreetMap contributors)

Beautiful waterfront homes and condominiums in Zihuatanejo

Along the waterfront in Zihuatanejo

Along the Fisherman's Path in Zihuatanejo

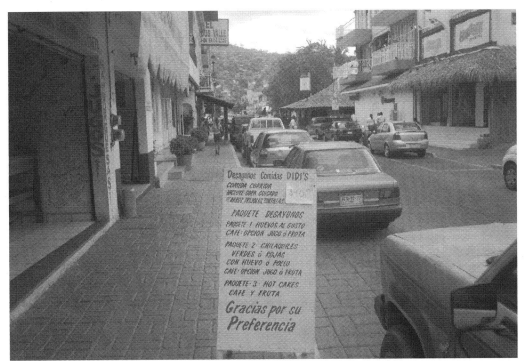

The main shopping street in Zihuatanejo

The colorful craft market in Zihuatanejo

On the beach in Ixtapa

In the town center of modern Ixtapa

On the remote beach of La Soledad, a half-day outing from Zihuatanejo

The small isolated fishing village of La Soledad

The countryside surrounding Ixtapa and Zihuatanejo

The making of roof tiles by hand in a local village outside Zihuatanejo

MANZANILLO, COLIMA

Manzanillo is not a common port of call on Panama Canal itineraries. Only a few cruise ships call in on this port of call, which is a relatively busy container port with most of the traffic handled for Guadalajara, México City and the central plateau region. The city of 100,000 has also become an important tourist destination because of its many beautiful beaches. Over the past two decades, numerous beautiful hotels have been developed and as a result, the city has a major airport with flights connecting Manzanillo to many U. S. cities.

Manzanillo is located south of Puerto Vallarta in the Mexican state of Colima, which is one of the smallest states in the country. The capital city also known as Colima is located inland from Manzanillo about a 1.5 hour drive. And just to the north of the capital is Pico de Colima, the most active volcano in all of México.

THE SETTING: The coastal area of Colima is relatively rugged with mountains seeming to rise out of the sea, there being little lowland fringing the Pacific. This is a region of intense beauty, especially inland where Pico de Colima rises as a perfectly shaped cone over 3,660 meters or 12,000 vertical feet, often seen with wisps of steam or ash billowing out of the crater.

This is a tropical landscape, more of a wet and dry savanna with a mix of shorter trees and open grasslands. At one time there was more standing timber, especially tropical hardwoods, but it has been used for furniture making and building over the centuries. There is a distinctive dry season during the winter months with summer having heavy rainfall, often augmented by the passage of hurricanes. The temperatures are generally in the 80's Fahrenheit, but summer can be very humid.

A BRIEF HISTORY: Alvaro de Saavedra first landed in what is now Manzanillo Bay in 1527. It became one more Pacific shipbuilding port for the trade across the Pacific to the Philippines. All during the period when riches from the Far East were coming across to Mexican ports there was a plague of Portuguese, French and British pirates. Having a port like Manzanillo gave the added advantage of another place in which to take shelter.

After Mexican independence, the present day port known as Manzanillo began to develop as an important Pacific access point to the central valley, the heart of the country. And by 1889, it was connected by rail to the capital city of Colima. And by 1908, the city had become an official port of entry with immigration and customs facilities.

All through the early 20th century, sport fishermen frequented Manzanillo, but its development of luxury resort hotels did not begin until the construction of Las Hadas in mid century. It will be remembered as the background location for the famous Hollywood movie "10."

VISITING MANZANILLO: Cruise ships dock in the Port of Manzanillo at the southern end of Manzanillo Bay adjacent to the old historic downtown area. The famous resort hotels like Las Hadas are located on the Santiago Peninsula, a rather hilly and rocky thumb of land that separates the port area from Bahía de Santiago where all the beautiful residential areas are located. The only assured way of seeing the hotels and scenic beaches is to either participate in one of the ship's city tours or have a private car and driver/guide arranged by your cruise line. Once again I do caution against using local taxi services that have not been pre arranged for you.

A few ships may offer an all day tour to the city of Colima, and to the base of the Colima volcano, especially if there is any eruptive activity that can be viewed closer up than from the city. When Colima volcano is in an eruptive state, it is an awesome spectacle.

There are no major monuments, great cathedrals or important museums, as this is essentially a commercial port combined with a tourist oriented beach resort. I recommend the following two major attractions in the Manzanillo area apart from the various beautiful beaches:
* The full-day tour to Pico de Colima, the most active volcano in the country. It is spectacular, often snow covered during winter unless it is erupting large quantities of ash and cinder bombs. The journey is worth the effort if you are one who appreciates spectacular scenery, and if you also have a sense of adventure.
* Centro Manzanillo - Taking a stroll down the Malecón, seeing the big sailfish statue and visiting the shops in the city center is worth a bit of time. It does make you realize that there is an actual small commercial district and that Manzanillo is more than just hotels and beaches.

DINING OUT: Given the nature of the one-day port call, lunch will be the only meal you could have away from the ship without being on an all-day tour. Unfortunately the ship docks in the port area of Old Manzanillo. All of the good restaurants that I would want to recommend are scattered around the city and without a private car, you cannot access them since taxi service is not to be relied upon unless previously arranged. If your ship offers a shuttle bus to Las Hadas, then you can have a good lunch at any of the restaurants inside the hotel, as the standards are all maintained at a five-star level.

SHOPPING: You will find the same types of arts and crafts or souvenir items to buy in Manzanillo as you saw in Zihuatanejo or Acapulco. There are no specific shops that I feel comfortable to recommend, as they are all so similar. Those not offering the souvenir items or some genuine crafts are selling resort clothing, jewelry and liquor, as these are what appeal to most vacationers.

FINAL NOTES" In many ways it is a shame that you will be visiting Manzanillo by ship because the dock area is so far away from the parts of the city that are truly oriented toward tourism. Other than going on a city tour offered through the cruise line or ordering a private car with a driver/guide, there is no easy way to get around Manzanillo because it is quite spread out. And all the good restaurants I would want to recommend are too scattered around the urban area that attempting to go to just one without a prearranged taxi would not be wise.

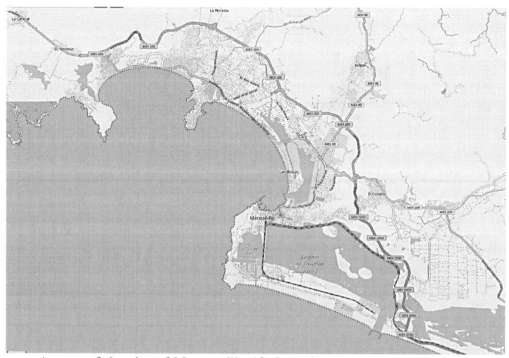

A map of the city of Manzanillo (© OpenStreetMap contributors)

The famous Las Hadas Hotel in Manzanillo (Work of Yaomautzin Ohtokani Olvera Lara, CC BY SA 3.0, Wikimedia.org)

In the downtown of Old Manzanillo (Work of I Tatehuari, CC BY SA 3.0, Wikimedia.org)

Fishermen cleaning fish on the docks in Old Manzanillo

On Playa Santiago (Work of Yaomautzin Ohtokani Olivera Lara, CC BY SA 3.0, Wikimedia.org)

PUERTO VALLARTA, JALISCO

In 1964, when a Hollywood studio decided to film the Tennessee Williams play, "A Night of the Iguana" in Puerto Vallarta, few in the United States had heard of this obscure village on the west coast of México. The film, starring Richard Burton, Ava Gardner and Deborah Kerr was dazzling even though it was made in black and white. The exotic setting of the small Mexican town nestled against thickly forested hills was captivating to audiences. And many people wanted to try and visit this sleepy and remote town. Today more than half a century later, Puerto Vallarta is connected to major cities in the United States and Canada by direct jet service, and its shoreline is home to modern high-rise hotels and condos. It is an international destination, the new Acapulco in that it has become the most fashionable and favored of all the Pacific beach resorts. With 255,000 residents, it has become the second largest city in the state of Jalisco after the capital of Guadalajara. And you must consider that the most northern suburban development of Nuevo Vallarta has over 115,000 people, but it is not figured into the metropolitan figures because it is across the border in the state of Nayarit. Thus greater Puerto Vallarta has 370,000 residents in total.

THE SETTING: Puerto Vallarta occupies a narrow coastal plain beneath the Sierra Madre Occidental, that wall of mountains that runs along the west coast of the country to where it intersects the transverse range just south of Puerto Vallarta. This gives the city a narrow escape from the volcanic and tectonic zone that lies a short distance to the south in the neighboring state of Colima. However, small earthquakes can and do occur in the area of Puerto Vallarta and the potential for feeling the effects of a major tremor in the mountains is quite high.

Modern Puerto Vallarta consists of several distinctive zones. These include:
* The Old City - Located in the southern part of the greater urban area, the Old City is the heart of the original fishing village. It has narrow, cobbled streets and traditional architecture that gives it a very colonial flavor
* Zona Romantica - South of the Old City and the Rio Cuale is one of the beautiful sections of the city, built into the hills and containing many of the

earliest of the vacation homes built after the tourist discovery of the area.

* Hotel Zone - This is the waterfront area north of the Old City where high-rise development is crowding along the shoreline in the way that Acapulco developed during the 20th century.

* Residential Zone - Behind the Hotel Zone is an extensive residential area that extends along the coastal plain and into the foothills at a point where the lowland is at is widest.

* Nuevo Vallarta - North of the airport and across the Ameca River and the state boundary into Nayarit is the newest area to be developing

The climate is tropical, with temperatures in the upper 80's to low 90's much of the year. But the rainfall regime is one of intense summer thundershowers in what is essentially a monsoonal pattern. Although winter is dry, occasional light thundershowers can occur on an infrequent basis. Thus the winter months have become the most favored among tourists, giving the city a seasonal basis with one economic high and one low every year. During late summer, occasional hurricanes will track along the coast and once in a while cause severe damage to Puerto Vallarta.

SETTLEMENT HISTORY: Many visitors that come to Puerto Vallarta confine their stay to the Hotel Zone, seeing a very modern and vibrant landscape and they do not realize that this city has a colonial history. Long before tourism, Puerto Vallarta was an active fishing village, service center for farmers living in the Ameca River valley and for miners working claims in the Sierra Nevada Occidental to the east.

As far back as 1524, Hernán Cortés explored the Ameca River valley and battled the native tribes that defended it. The bay into which the river flows is named Bahia Banderas for the colorful banners that the native people carried into battle. The bay was charted and mariners knew that in times of bad weather they could take refuge here, yet no major settlement occurred. During the 18th century the small settlement known as Las Peñas served as a small smuggling port for goods destined inland to the mining and agricultural towns of San Sebastian del Oeste and Mascota. By 1859, the government sold a large tract of land to the Camarena brothers from Guadalajara to develop the area into a major fishing and agricultural region to better serve the mines of the interior. The town grew steadily and in 1918 it officially became a municipality and was given the name Puerto Vallarta in honor of a former governor of Jalisco.

What initially slowed the development of the town was the fact that the land was company owned and could only be purchased at inflated values. After 1921, under new land reforms, a large segment was given ejido status, which meant the farmers owned it cooperatively, but could not sell the land to any outsiders. It took a local uprising in the late 1920's to ultimately bring about changes in the land ownership policies. As mining in the interior began to decline, many former miners sought agricultural land and slowly drifted down into the Ameca River valley looking to settle as farmers.

Until the early 1940's, this area around Puerto Vallarta remained isolated, accessible only by air, sea or by torturous roads from the interior. The roads were not negotiable by automobile, only mule or horse, and this stymied any modern development in Puerto Vallarta. But with its small plane air service, those tourists seeking out of the way locales in which to relax, and those in the arts and literary realm discovered Puerto Vallarta as a rare gem of a getaway. It would not, however, be until the 1960's that Puerto Vallarta would truly be discovered, after the government had clarified the policy of land use and ownership.

The major catalyst was the 1963 filming of "The Night of the Iguana," which focused so much attention on the beauty and remoteness of the locale. Part of the exposure was not generated directly by the movie, but rather by the press descending upon Puerto Vallarta because of the torrid relationship between its main star Richard Burton and Elizabeth Taylor, who was not his co-star at this time. Ava Gardner, another hot and sensual Hollywood star, was Burton's co-star.

After the success of the movie in generating interest, the government recognized the potential for development and invested in the expansion of the airport, improving highways and other city infrastructure. And it did not take long for tourism to begin to boom, and it has not stopped ever since. Access by air to American and Canadian cities today has made Puerto Vallarta one of the most favored of Mexican beach resorts. Yet it is still physically rather isolated in that the journey by road from Guadalajara is still long and not easily negotiated. Today the city is crowded with five-star hotel properties, condominiums, apartments and smaller resorts catering to a wide variety of price ranges. And of course the cruise ship industry has discovered Puerto Vallarta, making it a prime stop on Mexican west coast cruises or on longer itineraries en route to or from the Panama Canal.

WHAT TO DO WHILE VISITING: Most cruise lines have their ships spend one full day in Puerto Vallarta, but the five-star cruise lines on occasion offer itineraries where the stop is overnight. There are many interesting things to see and do in Puerto Vallarta, and on occasion the more upmarket cruise lines will offer a full-day air excursion to Guadalajara. Most cruise lines will offer extensive all-day and half-day tours of the city. The alternative is a private car with a driver/guide. Once again, I do not recommend taxis unless prearranged. Among the important sights in the city are:

* Zona Romantica - Just south of the Old City, this historic zone is the most popular in Puerto Vallarta, home to the beautiful basilica and many fine shops, restaurants and nightclubs, but it is the traditional architecture that makes this zone so special.

* Church of Our Lady of Guadalupe - The main basilica or cathedral for the city, noted for its metal crown atop the bell tower is the most photographed site in the city.

* Old Town - An historic district noted for its cobblestone streets that climb the hillsides, and for its authentic colonial architecture.

* El Centro - The downtown heart of the city, most noted for its fine quality art galleries and its art walks. It is also very traditional architecturally.

* El Malecón - The famous boardwalk along the ocean that runs from the Zona Romantica all the way up to the hotel district. The boardwalk is also lined with beautiful palm trees and is the place to see and be seen.

* Los Muertos Pier - The primary fishing pier leading off El Malecón, and it affords good views of the city skyline.

* Vallarta Botanical Gardens - A lush tropical garden featuring the vegetation of the Pacific coastal region. Open 9 AM to 6 PM daily.

* Bucerias and Nuevo Vallarta - Two small towns north of the city where there is a lot of new development. Here there are plenty of shops and restaurants, but in a quiet atmosphere.

Puerto Vallarta is also known for its beautiful beaches that figure prominently into the tourist draw. The major beaches to see include:

* Garza Blanca - This is the primary city beach.

* Punta de Mita - This is the beautiful sandy beach at the tip of the Bahia Banderas.

* Playa de los Muertos - Here us one of the more popular beaches close in to the city center.

* Playa las Animas - Located south of the city, but only accessible by boat, this is one of the more hidden gems of the area.

* Playa las Gemelas - This is another hidden gem of a beach, famous for its soft white sands.

There are also numerous special attractions around Puerto Vallarta, but on a one-day visit, it may be difficult to find a tour offered by your cruise line that will include one of these sites:

*Las Caletas Beach - Well outside of the city, this is an excellent site for whale watching, but it requires a private taxi ride or a tour in order to visit on a one-day port call.

* Paradise Adventure Park - A chance for a canopy walk in the rain forest, but again this requires a trip out of the city or to be part of a tour

* Canopy Bay - For those who want a zip line adventure in the rainforest, this is the place to visit.

Outside of the city, there is the possibility of two all-day tours depending upon the cruise line. These are:

* A Visit to Colonial San Sebastian - This is generally an all day tour by coach, taking you up into the Sierra Madre Occidental to San Sebastian. Here you will visit one of the beautifully preserved colonial mining towns of the mountains that parallel the west coast. Lunch is normally included on this tour, which gets you out into some of the wild country of the interior.

* A charter flight to and visit in the city of Guadalajara. With over 6,000,000 residents, Guadalajara is the second largest city in the country. It is known for its well preserved Centro, the historic core of the city that still retains most of the great colonial buildings that made it such a beloved place to visit for those who savor the beauty of Colonial México. The second greatest feature of a visit to Guadalajara is its famous arts and crafts district in the historic and traditional suburb of Tlaquepaque.

Whatever you decide to do, even if it is just a quiet walk in the Old City or the downtown area, you will find Puerto Vallarta to be beautiful and inviting. However, be aware that during the winter months, the city becomes quite crowded with foreign tourists. On days when there are two or more cruise ships in port; you can expect even larger crowds at popular venues.

DINING OUT: There are literally hundreds of restaurants in Puerto Vallarta, but you are faced with two problems. Firstly you are only there for a single day unless you are fortunate enough to be staying overnight, and secondly the restaurants are scattered all over the urban area. I am recommending restaurants that are open for lunch and that are in the old city center where most ships will have a shuttle drop stop. My recommendations are few in number, as the majority of the really good restaurants are only open for dinner:

* Layla's Restaurant - At Venezuela #137, Contraesquina Parque Hidalgo and open from 9 AM to 11 PM. This is a very popular and traditional Mexican restaurant with both good food and atmosphere. However, it is about 1.5 miles north of the old city center area where shuttles will drop off guests. But if you walk along the waterfront you will find it relaxing and have cool breezes.

* La Palapa - At Pulpito #105-3 on the beach at Playa Los Muertos, and open from 8:30 AM to 11:30 PM, this is an outstanding traditional Mexican

restaurant that has a Jalisco twist to its menu.

If your ship is staying into the evening and you wish to go to dinner, ask the shore concierge or local tourist representative to book a taxi pick up at the ship and return for specific times. Here are two outstanding dinner choices, but reservations are necessary:
* Vista Grill - Overlooking the old central city at Pulpito #377 and open from 5:30 to 11:30 PM, this restaurant offers superb dinners with a Mexican flair and it also has a fantastic view, especially at sunset. I highly recommend it.
* Cafedesartistes - At Guadalupe Sanches #740 and open from 6 to 11:30 PM, this is one of the most highly rated restaurants in Puerto Vallarta. The cuisine is more European with a French and Continental touch. The food and service are both superb.

SHOPPING: Unlike the ports visited thus far, shopping here for arts and hand crafts is a bit difference. In the state of Jalisco there is a very strong artistic tradition. One of the prize gift items is to bring back a piece of lacquered wood trays, round dishes or bowls. They are generally black and have floral designs painted in vivid colors. Jalisco is also known for its fine woven cloth and rugs, and it is famous for its hand blown glassware. In Puerto Vallarta here are a few of the major reputable shops:
* Old Town Farmer's Market - Located in Lazaro Cardenas Park in the city center, and open from 9:30 AM to 2 PM, this is a great open bazaar of all types of craft items and foods. It is a bit of a walk from the very center of the city where most cruise lines will have a shuttle drop off.
* Lucy's CuCu Cabana - In the city center at Basilio Badillo #295, and open from 10 AM to 6 PM, this shop specializes in a wide variety of handmade and traditional art objects, especially colorful figurines and dolls.
* Mundo de Cristal - At Esquina de Insrgentes and Basillio Badillo in the city center and open from 9 AM to 7 PM, this is essentially a shop that specializes in the well-known Mexican glassware and also lacquered wood.
* Señor Talavera - Located at Calle Encino #275 just across the Rio Cuale from the very heart of town, this shop specializes in the elegant hand painted Talavera pottery. Open daily 10 AM to 8 PM, closing 4 PM Sunday.

VISITING GUADALAJARA: If you are cruising on one of the very high end lines, there is a possibility of a visit to the country's second largest and most beautiful city - Guadalajara. The barrier of the Sierra Madre Occidental range makes a bus tour to Guadalajara impossible, as given the state of the roads, it would take six to eight hours just to get there. Thus the only way such a visit can be accomplished is by use of a small charter aircraft. This means the tour will be quite expensive when you factor in a shuttle bus to and from the Puerto

Vallarta Airport, the charter flight and a tour bus in Guadalajara. But if you are interested in Mexican history and architecture as well as traditional arts and crafts, this is the trip for you providing it is even offered. I have made the trip several times and found it to be absolutely captivating. It takes about 1.5 hours to fly utilizing a small single or double engine prop aircraft. But if a tour is organized to depart no later than 8:30 AM from the airport, it can arrive in Guadalajara by 10 AM. And if the return journey is made after 7 PM, it allows nine hours to tour the city.

Guadalajara is a large city with a metro area population of around 6,000,000. It prides itself in having a very large and well-maintained central core that contains some of the most beautiful churches and government buildings in the entire country, many dating back to the 1600's. And in addition to the historic district, there is the suburban community of Tlaquepaque, which is noted for being both an historic town, but also home to many artists' studios and workshops. And if time permits, there is also the very modern and up market suburban zone of Zapopan, one of the most fashionable and modern districts of any Mexican city.

It is unlikely that most of you who read this book will have a chance to visit Guadalajara on your west coast cruise, but I offer this note in the rare event your cruise line does offer such an excursion. It can be an exhausting day, but it gives you a chance to see the country's most famous city for both its architecture and artistic enterprises. And perhaps if you are lucky enough to visit, your lunch stop will include some genuine mariachi music, which was first created in Guadalajara.

FINAL NOTES: Over the years Puerto Vallarta has become a major city complete with high-rise hotels and heavy traffic. But the old city still has the romantic flavor that people expect even though it is somewhat commercialized. Unlike Acapulco, Puerto Vallarta is still fresh and has a great vibe that brings people back time after time. And fortunately the drug violence that has plagued Acapulco has not been a factor here. The city is quite safe during the day, but precaution when going out at night is always recommended anywhere in the country.

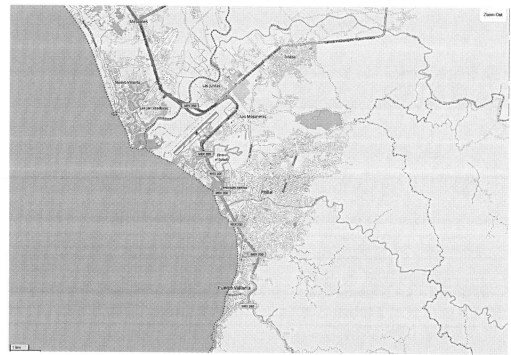

A map of Puerto Vallarta (© OpenStreetMap contributors)

A map of the Puerto Vallarta resort area (© OpenStreetMap contributors)

A map of old Puerto Vallarta (© OpenStreetMap contributors)

The modern beachfront and high-rise hotels and condominiums

197

Flying over the new residential areas of Puerto Vallarta

The massive hotel and condominium development is dramatic from the air

The waterfront of new Puerto Vallarta is filled with high-rises

These modern buildings detract from the old charm of Puerto Vallarta

The beautiful old historic cathedral (Work of KABAYEK, CC BY SA 3.0, Wikimedia.org)

Downtown old Puerto Vallarta (Work of Romarzur, CC BY SA 4.0, Wikimedia.org)

Downtown in old Puerto Vallarta

A map of central Guadalajara (© OpenStreetMap contributors)

Over the rooftops of central Guadalajara

The Palacio del Gobierno de Jalisco in Guadalajara

In Plaza de Armas in central Guadalajara

The great Catedral de Guadalajara and the eastern plaza

The main plaza in Tlaquepaque

Colorful street vendors at the plaza in Tlaquepaque

Street vendors sell many basic staples for the home

CABO SAN LUCAS,
BAJA CALIFORNIA SUR

Either the first or last port of call on most cruises that transit the Panama Canal, Cabo San Lucas is one of the most popular resort cities visited in México. Some cruises that leave eastbound out of Los Angeles, San Francisco or Vancouver will on occasion first stop for a day in San Diego, California. But all, however, stop in Cabo San Lucas. Many passengers consider it to be their most favored stop within México because it is very clean, modern and exceptionally safe. There is very little poverty since both Cabo San Lucas and San José del Cabo live for tourism and jobs are plentiful. This prevents the typical barrios that you see everywhere else in México. Another reason for the lack of barrios or major crime is the isolation of these two resort cities. They are at the southern tip of the arid Baja California Peninsula, over 1,000 road miles from the border of the United States and cut off from the rest of México by the Gulf of California, or what the Mexicans call the Sea of Cortés.

Greater Los Cabos is actually two cities, Cabo San Lucas and San José del Cabo, separated by around 40 kilometers or 25 miles of strikingly beautiful coastline that is today lined with many new beach resort developments. Today the combined population of both cities is 287,000, the majority being foreigners or wealthy Mexicans who have chosen to retire or own vacation property here. Neither city has docking facilities adequate for cruise ships, but the waters at Cabo San Lucas are more sheltered and thus make for easier anchorage with tenders operating all day to take guests to shore and returning to the ship. Coach tours then operate to enable those who wish to explore a chance to visit San José del Cabo for either a half-day or full day's tour.

LAND'S END: The region of Los Cabos is often called Land's End because it is the southernmost tip of the1,600 kilometer or 1,000 mile long Baja California Peninsula. This relatively narrow strip of highly mountainous land is the result of the separation by the Gulf of California of the peninsula from the mainland. Underneath the gulf lies the great San Andreas Fault, a plate boundary between the Pacific and North American Plates. And as a result earthquake activity often occurs deep under the sea in the gulf, or on occasion along one of the lesser fault lines of the peninsula or mainland. The potential for catastrophic events haunts this area with its ever-present danger, yet development is continuing at a rapid pace.

The Baja Peninsula represents what is referred to as coastal desert. Very cold upwelling in the sea combined with the descending air out of the great Pacific High Pressure Zone inhibits significant precipitation, thus creating a desert environment. Occasional winter storms coming off the Pacific will brush the northern end of the peninsula, and summer monsoonal showers will occur at higher elevations during the summer months. And every few years, a tropical Pacific hurricane may sweep into the Gulf of California, bringing havoc in its wake.

The highest elevation on the peninsula reaches 10,157 feet and does have limited stands of pine forest. But the major portion of the peninsula exhibits a desert landscape, and it contains many distinctive species of cactus and other succulents along with occasional bursts of wildflowers in spring. Temperatures during summertime can soar to over 37 degrees Celsius or 100 degrees Fahrenheit and during winter inland temperatures can drop below freezing in the early morning hours. The desert exhibits the same visual characteristics as the southern deserts of Arizona and the Mexican state of Sonora, but there are significant differences in the vegetation species.

The peninsula is divided into two separate Mexican states. Baja California represents the northern half and is quite heavily populated along the United States border. Tijuana, the largest city, has a population of over 1,400,000 and the state capital of Mexicali has a population of just over 1,000,000. Tijuana is a popular tourist center for day trips, but to the south is Ensenada, the most northerly of the Mexican Pacific beach resorts. Mexicali is in the Imperial Valley, a rich irrigated agricultural zone supplied by the lower Colorado River. The southern half of the peninsula is within the state of Baja California del Sur, isolated by mostly unsettled desert tracts extending south from its northern neighbor, and connected by only one major paved road. The state's population is under 715,000 with just over 215,000 in the capital port city of La Paz and 287,000 in Los Cabos. Baja California del Sur is more arid than its northern counterpart, yet more exposed to the potential for hurricane damage, as occurred in Los Cabos in late summer 2014.

A BRIEF HISTORY: Prior to the coming of the Spanish, the native inhabitants of the peninsula were primarily primitive hunters and gatherers. The famous Hernán Cortés explored and actually named the Gulf of California in 1535, but found the region totally unworthy of development. He did name the gulf as Mar de Cortés, a somewhat egotistical gesture, but to this day the Mexican maps show it by that name and not as the Gulf of California.

Prior to the first Spanish mission being established in this region, pirates, including the notorious British privateer Sir Francis Drake, used the waters of Cabo San Lucas to loot Spanish ships. And it was this activity that led to the development of a mission outpost.

Spanish missionaries did establish a few missions along the gulf coast farther north, but in 1730, two priests did establish a mission at what is today San José del Cabo. The town was not established until the early 1820's, mainly as a resupply station for the Acapulco-Manila transoceanic traffic, which ended with the Mexican war for independence from Spain.

During the Mexican American War and later during the revolution against Diaz, only minor skirmishes took place in the remote southern portions of the Baja California Peninsula. During much of the 20th century, this area remained a backwater. There was not even a completed road between Cabo San Lucas and San José del Cabo until 1970. It was not until the Mexican government began to help in the development of a tourist infrastructure that Los Cabos began to attract foreign visitors in any significant number. And the progress has been phenomenal. Today the region is one of the most popular destinations in the country. Direct air services link it to many cities in the United States, especially in the American West. And a fully paved road now connects Los Cabos to La Paz and northward to Tijuana or Mexicali and the United States. Few people make the drive, as it is approximately 1,000 miles of empty desert with few places where a visitor can find lodging or refreshment. But it does enable supplies to come directly to Los Cabos for provisioning the many hotels and the construction industry.

Los Cabos has become a popular destination year around despite the summer desert heat. With air conditioning and cooling breezes blowing off the surrounding waters, summer is relatively comfortable. Many expatriates have chosen to retire in Los Cabos, as it now has all the major amenities North Americans could want. There are elegant shopping malls, major supermarkets and adequate medical facilities. And given its isolated location, Los Cabos has not become a location for major drug smuggling activities and has remained relatively free of violence. The normal street crime found on the mainland is also not a significant factor here because of the high degree of employment.

One of the major factors of concern with the development of tourism is the lack of significant environmental protection. The deserts of Baja California are fragile despite their formidable appearance. The Mexican government has been slow to respond to environmental concerns raised from outside of the country. There is a need for safeguards to protect the desert from being overly exploited by developers in the Los Cabos region and elsewhere in spots where foreign visitors are choosing to exploit.

WHAT TO DO WHILE VISITING: Los Cabos is known for its stunning beaches, its surfing, sailing, sport fishing and whale watching. Water plays the major role in the activities people come for. Cabo San Lucas is relatively modern and has little if any historic features. San José del Cabo has developed its old town core along historic lines since it at least dates back to the late colonial era. There are not many significant historic monuments, but its plaza and church along with a few surrounding buildings do give the city a degree of Mexican charm with a level of authenticity. But even the major portions of San José del Cabo are relatively new and oriented toward the visitor.

There are no port facilities in San José del Cabo, but Cabo San Lucas does have a small harbor that accommodates fishing and pleasure craft. Nowhere are there docking facilities for a cruise ship. Thus it is necessary for ships to anchor in the sheltered bay off Cabo San Lucas and then establish a tender service to ferry guests to and from the small harbor.

If you choose to not participate in any of your ship's excursions, the landing site for the tenders will place you right in the heart of Cabo San Lucas. Numerous restaurants, shops and local vendors are right within the confines of the small harbor. And at the far end, about a three-block walk from the landing, you will find the city's very upmarket mall. It is easy to spend the day simply exploring the heart of Cabo San Lucas. But of course you will miss out on seeing some of the beauties of the region and visiting San José del Cabo, which is a pleasant experience.

There are tours offered by your cruise line that will either focus on Cabo San Lucas or take you to San José del Cabo for a half-day excursion. Of course your cruise line can also arrange a private car with a driver/guide. And in this port I do feel it is safe to hire a local taxi, as keeping tourists safe and content is critical to the survival of the economy. Among the activities and sights to see in greater Los Cabos, here are my recommendations:
* Los Arcos - Also known as Land's End, this grouping of rocks is the southernmost tip of the Baja California Peninsula. You will see it from your anchored ship, but there are small excursion craft that will take you around the very tip of the peninsula, often chartered for group excursions by your cruise line.
* Lover's Beach - For those who want to spend time enjoying a romantic, but

often crowded strip of sand, this is the place. Lover's Beach is a sandbar that connects the inner gulf side of Cabo San Lucas with the open Pacific Ocean, you can hire a small motor launch to take you here for a romantic few hours.

* Old Town San José del Cabo - Both the drive to and from San José del Cabo and a walk around the plaza and back streets of the old town makes for a nice few hours of romantic sightseeing. This is one of the most popular and well patronized of the tours offered by the cruise lines.

* Cactimundo Garden - Located in San José del Cabo, this is quite a beautiful and well-developed cactus garden that exhibits the variety of cacti found in the North American deserts. Remember that cacti are only native to the Americas.

Among the many beaches to be visited apart from Lover's Beach, these are the recommended venues, but generally they are not included on the basic Los Cabos tours. The only way to visit one or more beaches is either by special excursion to a or by using local taxis:

* Chileno Beach in Cabo San Lucas - This is a very quiet and tranquil strip of sand with calm waters, numerous rock outcrops and a variety of marine life that can be seen by snorkeling.

* Santa Maria Beach in Cabo San Lucas - This is another white sandy strip with excellent snorkeling and beautiful surroundings that is quite popular.

* Cannery Beach in Cabo San Lucas - A quiet beautiful beach close to the harbor, yet still quite pristine with good snorkeling potential where you can easily spend the day.

* Playa Hotelera in San José del Cabo - Despite being lined with numerous hotels, the beach is public property. It is a bit difficult to access without going through one of the hotels, but it is beautiful and tranquil. The surf can be a bit rough at high tide, but at low tide it is great for walking. To reach it, you would need a private car or you can hire a taxi.

* Playa Palmilla in San José del Cabo - This sheltered beach is excellent for swimming and snorkeling, and it is generally not overly crowded.

There are a few important natural sights that can be seen in the Los Cabos area, but unless your cruise line happens to have a tour to one of them, you will need to make private arrangements by having the cruise line arrange a car and driver/guide or negotiating with a local taxi driver. Remember that here the local taxis are quite reliable and reasonably safe, as most drivers do speak English. My recommendations are:

* José Estuary and Bird Sanctuary - Located at the estuary of the San José River, this sanctuary does provide a home for many local bird species. It is not, however, well protected from horses or cattle being able to graze, and it was also battered by the 2014 hurricane.

* Socorro Island - You will need to take a local small craft from the marina in

Cabo San Lucas to visit this offshore island where you can dive and swim with dolphins, a variety of fish, mantas and some species of shark. There are several operators who provide service for those looking for some maritime adventure.

* Desert Park Natural Reserve - Here is a chance to see some of the open desert north of Cabo San Lucas, touring in old military trucks, but well guided. And during the winter months you can look out to see and spot humpback whales as they swim in these waters during their breeding season. If your cruise line cannot arrange it, you will find their representative in the docking area of Cabo San Lucas.

There are many other beaches and natural sites to visit in Los Cabos, but given that you have only a few hours of actual onshore time, I believe that the highlights I have recommended will suffice to keep you busy. And many who visit off of a cruise ship will plan to return at some time in the future for a holiday devoted just to this port of call.

DINING OUT: Depending upon the length of your stay, you may have time for lunch in Cabo San Lucas, but unless you are out with a private car and driver/guide, lunch in San José del Cabo is not possible given the 35-mile distance. Few cruise ships ever spend more than six to eight hours anchored off Cabo San Lucas. Thus my dining recommendations are only for Cabo San Lucas, and are as follows:

* Hacienda Cocina y Cantina - Located on Calle Gomez Farias facing the beach just opposite where the tenders dock. Medano Beach is not far, but walking is rather difficult because of all the various streets you will need to navigate, so take a taxi. This very popular restaurant by the sea opens at 8 AM and is open until 10 PM. It has outstanding lunches with an emphasis upon fresh seafood prepared with Mexican flair and zest. It is a bit expensive, but worth it.

* Omega Sports Bar and Grill - On the water at Medano Beach and Paseo del Pescador, a very popular venue for great Mexican food, but served in the less sedate atmosphere of a hip sports bar and cantina.

* Mariscos la Palmita - At 16 de Septiembre Street north of the main city center, so take a taxi. This is a very special seafood restaurant serving local fresh fish and shrimp prepared with Mexican spices and sauces, or simply grilled. It is open for lunch and dinner, but no specific hours are given. It has an excellent local reputation.

* Cabo Blue - Just off the harbor at Boulevard Marina #30, a short walk from the ship tender dock, and open from 10 AM to 4 PM, this is an excellent restaurant, but also a popular indoor-outdoor bar noted for its drinks, featuring tequila. But their Mexican cuisine is excellent.

SHOPPING: Cabo San Lucas and San José del Cabo offer excellent shopping for both handcraft items with genuine Mexican flavor and also fine quality Mexican furniture that can be shipped to your home by very reliable furniture dealers. And in Cabo San Lucas the major shopping mall features many exquisite shops for clothing and jewelry for those who are interested in this type of shopping. Here are my recommendations for fine quality Mexican crafts:

* Arte de Origen - At the Puerto Paraiso Mall, store #46 in Cabo San Lucas, this is an outstanding store featuring handmade creations and traditional home furnishings. Open 10 AM to 7 PM daily.

* Vitrofusion Glass Blowing Factory - At Calle Cabo San Lucas, a short distance by walking from the small harbor, this glass blowing workshop uses recycled glass to make incredibly beautiful vases, figurines and larger objects. They will also customize anything you request. Tours are given daily from 9 AM to 2 PM.

* Paquime Gallery - In San José del Cabo at Calle Alvaro Obregon #17, this small shop features traditional pottery, woodcarvings and a variety of handmade treasures that are sure to please. Open 9 AM to 5 PM daily.

FINAL NOTES: I personally find Cabo San Lucas too Americanized for my taste. You hardly realize you are really in México. I much prefer San José del Cabo, as it at least does have a bit of Mexican history represented in its central core. But even here the hotels are ultra new and modern and the whole atmosphere is one of catering to the visitor. I feel that this area does do a great service to the country in that it enables people unfamiliar with México to develop a bit of a feel for the country in an atmosphere that is not as foreign as you would find in the older, more established cities. And being almost crime free, it helps visitors forget about the drug violence that plagues the rest of the country. Along with this, there is the beauty of the beaches and the desert mountains that serve as a dramatic backdrop.

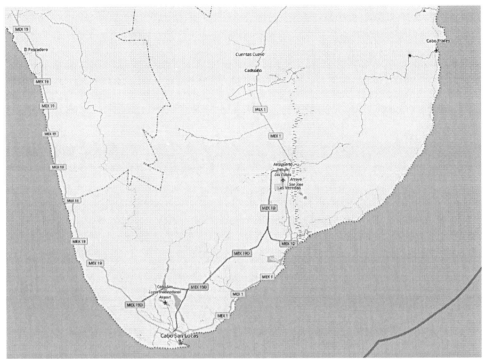

The tip of the Baja Peninsula (© OpenStreetMap contributors)

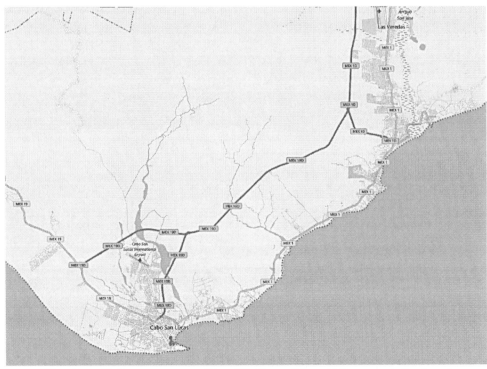

The Los Cabos communities (© OpenStreetMap contributors)

A map of Cabo San Lucas (© OpenStreetMap contributors)

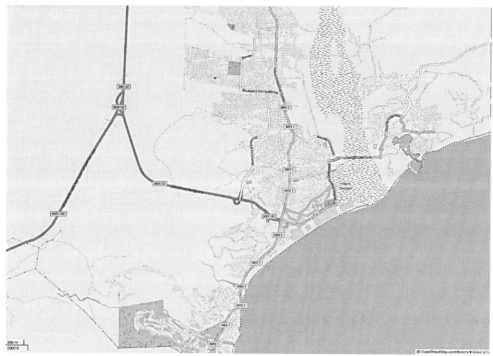

A map of San José del Cabo (© OpenStreetMap contributors)

The shoreline of Cabo San Lucas

The landing for cruise ship tenders in Cabo San Lucas

The Cabo San Lucas harbor filled with pleasure craft

In the heart of downtown Cabo San Lucas

The elegant Puerto Paraiso Mall in Cabo San Lucas

Land's End for the Baja California Peninsula

Los Arcos is a popular Land's End natural feature

A small portion of Lover's Beach

On the main plaza of San José del Cabo

The old mission church in San José del Cabo

Street color in downtown San José del Cabo

The Cactimundo Gardens in San José del Cabo

FINAL WORDS

This brings the journey to its conclusion. I have covered the major ports of call on a voyage between the east and west coast of the United States with the transit through the incredible Panama Canal. As I noted earlier, there are variations as to the length and itinerary of each cruise offered by the various companies operating through the canal. In the spring, some cruise lines offer a relocation cruise when they are moving their ships from Florida to Alaska, and it is possible to book multiple segments and end up in Vancouver where the Alaska cruises primarily begin. Or in the autumn you may book a repositioning cruise from Vancouver to Florida or all the way north and down the St. Lawrence River to Montréal. And during the Northern Hemisphere winter months, there are cruises between Florida and the west coast of South America. And all pass through the Panama Canal.

A very few cruise lines offer ports of call that I have not covered in this traveler's companion book simply because they are so seldom visited. After looking at the itineraries for the major lines, I chose the ports of call that are most heavily visited. I trust this book will become a valuable companion for those of you who do decide to book a cruise through the Panama Canal. This great waterway now entering its second century is one of the true engineering marvels of the world. And in another year when the larger second set of locks is complete, it will become an even more vital link in global communication. And this new addition will enable some of the mega cruise ships to now start offering itineraries that will include a transit through the Panama Canal, something they are not able to offer at present.

I have cruised the Panama Canal four times and the Suez Canal twice. There is no comparison, as the Suez Canal is a totally open sea level canal without need for any surge protection gates. Your ship simply sails in and for all practical purposes it looks like you are sailing into the opening of a large river. And the passage takes over eight to 10 hours with no change in scenery. The Panama Canal is dramatic with its massive locks and their huge steel doors. There is a sense of drama in watching how your ship enters the system and proceeds through the locks. And the surrounding lush rainforest environment of Panama adds a sense of beauty to the overall experience.

When you take your cruise, I hope you will be able to marvel at this great wonder now in its second century of operation with much the same equipment still in use. It is truly one of the major creations of modern mankind.

ABOUT THE AUTHOR

Dr. Lew Deitch

I am Canadian and a semi-retired professor of geography with over 46 years of teaching experience. During my distinguished career, I directed the Honors Program at Northern Arizona University and developed many programs relating to the study of contemporary world affairs. I am an honors graduate of The University of California, Los Angeles, earned my Master of Arts at The University of Arizona and completed my doctorate in geography at The University of New England in Australia. I am a globetrotter, having visited 92 countries on all continents except Antarctica. My primary focus is upon human landscapes, especially such topics as local architecture, foods, clothing and folk music. I am also a student of world politics and conflict.

I enjoy being in front of an audience, and have spoken to thousands of people at civic and professional organizations. I have been lecturing on board ships for a major five star cruise line since 2008.

I love to introduce people to exciting new places both by means of presenting vividly illustrated talks and through serving as a tour consultant for ports of call. I am also an avid writer, and for years I have written my own text books used in my university classes. Now I have turned my attention to writing travel companions, books that will introduce you to the country you are visiting, but not serving as a touring book like the major guides you find in all of the bookstores.

I also love languages, and my skills include a conversational knowledge of German, Russian and Spanish.

I am proudly Canadian-American and have lived in British Columbia and Australia during my teaching career. Arizona has been his permanent home since 1974. One exciting aspect of my life was the ten-year period, during which I volunteered my time as an Arizona Highway Patrol reserve trooper, working out on the streets and highways and also developing new safety and enforcement programs for use statewide. I presently live just outside of Phoenix in the beautiful resort city of Scottsdale and still offer a few courses for the local community colleges when I am at home.

I would like to extend an invitation for you to join me on one of the Silversea cruise segments when I am on board presenting my destination talks. You would find it to be a wonderful experience, especially after having read my book on this area, or on the others I have written about.

FOR MORE INFORMATION REGARDING TRAVELING
ON BOARD WHEN I AM THE SPEAKER, CONTACT, WESTSIDE INTERNATIONAL TRAVEL, THE TRAVEL AGENCY I USE FOR ALL MY TRAVELS AT:

www.westsideintltravel.com

TO CONTACT ME, PLEASE CHECK OUT MY WEB PAGE
FOR MORE INFORMATION AT:
http://www.doctorlew.com

Made in the USA
Middletown, DE
18 July 2018